Sixty Shades of Love

Also by Darlene Matule

Under the Gallus Frame

Framework of a Family

Sixty Shades of Love

A Memoir

Darlene Matule

RESOURCE *Publications* • Eugene, Oregon

SIXTY SHADES OF LOVE
A Memoir

Copyright © 2018 Darlene Matule. All rights reserved. Except for brief quotations in critical publications or reviews, no part of this book may be reproduced in any manner without prior written permission from the publisher. Write: Permissions, Wipf and Stock Publishers, 199 W. 8th Ave., Suite 3, Eugene, OR 97401.

Resource Publications
An Imprint of Wipf and Stock Publishers
199 W. 8th Ave., Suite 3
Eugene, OR 97401

www.wipfandstock.com

PAPERBACK ISBN: 978-1-5326-3967-8
HARDCOVER ISBN: 978-1-5326-3968-5
EBOOK ISBN: 978-1-5326-3969-2

Manufactured in the U.S.A.

I dedicate this memoir to my dear husband, Steve.
We've been through the worst of times and the best of times. Together.
We met on a dance floor. We're still dancing.
After over sixty years, I am blessed to be able to say, "I'm married to my best friend."

"Great marriages don't happen
By luck or accident.
They are a result of a consistent
Investment of time, thoughtfulness,
Forgiveness, affection, prayer,
Mutual respect and a rock-solid
Commitment between a
Husband and wife."

Dave Willis

Chapter 1

"It's been sixty years since our first date," he exclaims.

"Sixty years? Impossible!"

And I remember... From April 15, 1955 to now. Dancing to dreading. Sunshine to snowstorms. And everything in between.

༄

We met on a dance floor.

How do I get rid of this guy? I wondered. At a college mixer, stuck dancing with a Central American foreign exchange student who smelled like he'd lived in his skintight chartreuse shirt for a month. Who'd been holding me possessively close for three dances.

I looked for an out.

His greasy friend still stood at the edge of the dance floor, undressing me with his eyes, drool edging down his chin. *Waiting for his turn?* I cringed, desperate to get away.

At the end of a two-step, I felt a new, larger hand on my shoulder. Heard a different voice ask, "Wanna dance?"

I turned. Saw his fingers reach for mine. Fingers I would soon learn could stop a 95 miles per hour baseball as it tore into third base. I moved toward him. Smelled the scent of Old Spice. Felt him put one hand on my waist as his other gently laced our fingers together.

To the strains of *I'm in the Mood for Love*, he expertly guided me across the dance floor.

When the music ended I hung onto my savior. Quickly, the band began a jitterbug. Before I could tell New Guy I didn't know how to fast dance, I found myself in the middle of the floor—dancing—having fun.

We danced together until the music stopped at midnight.

Thinking New Guy (I still didn't know his name—he hadn't asked me mine) would ask me out for a Coke, I was disappointed.

New Guy said, "My friend John is coming to pick me up. His wife's gone, and I promised to go to Luigi's with him after the mixer."

So much for that, I thought. But The Squeezer had disappeared. I thanked my lucky stars.

I went to 24 Flavors with some girlfriends, had a cherry milkshake, and went back to the dorm. I had a hard time falling asleep.

The next morning Margaret, an upper classman, stopped me at breakfast and asked about my "date."

"No date," I said. "Don't even know his name." I told her what New Guy had saved me from. We giggled.

"Just so you know for later," she said, "his name is Steve Matule. He's a junior at Gonzaga. Supercharged the baseball team last spring. Set a Gonzaga batting record. Nice guy."

Later that morning, I went downtown on the bus with some girlfriends. We had lunch. Shopped at The Crescent. I reveled in the whole floor of fabric available for my new project. (Back home in Montana I'd had to order special material from St. Louis or Seattle.) Then we saw Leslie Caron in the new movie, *The Glass Slipper*.

When I got back to the dorm, my phone was ringing.

"Hi, this is Steve Matule."

Glad I'd learned his name, I said, "Hi."

"How'd you like to go see Billy May with me tonight?"

Now, I was an unworldly, not quite nineteen-year-old college freshman. My only dates since I'd come to Spokane in September had been with my high school boyfriend who'd quit school at the end of the first semester and gone back home to Montana.

I asked, "Who's Billy May?"

For a full minute, I heard silence. Luckily, he patiently explained. "Billy May has a Big Band. He's playing tonight at Natatorium Park."

I wavered. I had full intention of beginning my long-put-off English project that Saturday night.

"I've got to start a term paper. I'm already late."

Another moment of silence.

Chapter 1

"We'd be going with your friend Midge Bird (a popular upper-classman) and Jerry Lehigh," he encouraged.

I took a big breath.

"What time?"

When he arrived at 7:30, I was wearing a royal blue taffeta dress and blue suede high heels.

We danced every dance. He twirled me around the floor. I followed his lead. Had the best time I'd ever had in my life.

After the music ended, Steve took us all to dinner. The service was slow.

"We're going to miss our deadline," Midge worried.

"No problem," Steve said. He called our house mother, Mrs. Smith, who said, "Have fun. I'll wait up for the girls."

My life changed that day—April 15, 1955.

Steve managed to see me at least a few minutes every day the next week. For a milkshake. A stroll through the Gonzaga campus. A milkshake. A walk down to the nearby Spokane River. A milkshake.

But by late that Saturday afternoon, Steve still hadn't called to invite me out that evening. *And I thought he was interested*, I agonized. I knew I was.

So when, at the last minute, my friend Monica asked if I'd be her boyfriend's brother's date to a Gonzaga mixer, I agreed. *Not much fun*, I told myself afterwards. The only good thing *that* night had been the root beer float my date bought me afterwards at the A&W.

The next morning I got an early phone call. "How about watching my baseball game today? Afterwards we can take a ride around town. I have John's car for the afternoon."

I watched the game. *Rather boring*. Enjoyed the car ride through the north side of Spokane.

As we were driving back to college down North Wall Street, we saw a sign.

Bern Thera Terrace—New Homes for Sale

I loved houses—had already been planning the dream home I'd move into someday. (Old Boyfriend had been drawing the floorplan for our first place when he decided to quit college.)

Steve and I walked through a two-bedroom model. Daffodils graced a clay pot by the front door. The kitchen had aqua steel cabinets—my favorite color. We both oohed and ahhed.

Steve dropped off John's car at Wes's Gas Station (where John worked part-time to feed his three kids and wife), and we took a side trip down by the river. On the way back to my dorm, we stood under a flowering tree for a moment. He bent toward me. Paused. Then kissed me right on the lips. It was magic.

I got back to my room, took out my Smith Corona portable, and began writing. Before dinner, I'd already finished the shell of my term paper. The words sped from my brain to my fingers and onto a blank sheet of paper—as fast as Morse code clicks turn into a telegram.

One evening after dinner Steve stopped by my dorm. "Wanna go for a walk?" he asked.

By that time, I was ready to go (almost) anywhere with the six-footer who was fast becoming more important to me than my studies.

We ambled down Boone Avenue toward Gonzaga, took a left in front of DeSmet Hall and another onto DeSmet Avenue. In those days there were one-family residences lining the north side of the street. As we walked by a story-and-a-half white house, a classmate of Steve's came out.

"Just want you to know I'll be voting for you tomorrow, Steve," the guy said.

"Thanks, I appreciate your support," my date replied.

And that was how I discovered Steve was running for Senior Class President.

Here I was—a mere freshman, so shy I had a hard time talking to people to whom I hadn't been formally introduced. And someone so popular he was in contention for one of the most prestigious offices in the college hierarchy was pursuing me.

Wow!

For the past couple of weeks I'd been cataloguing the qualifications I wanted in a husband. *Nothing like being prepared*, I'd told myself.

I thought of my parents' marriage.

My daddy was the best father! My girl-friends bragged about him to me. "He's so handsome!" Julia said. "He's so patient," Phyllis confided when

Chapter 1

Daddy dug her family car out of a snowdrift and never even raised his voice in the process.

But my mother was boss. She'd say "Jump" and he'd say "How high?"

Daddy wasn't hen-pecked. Just selfless.

Being in a love-hate relationship with my mother, I decided I wanted a "take charge" husband. Did I see a lot of my mother in myself and want to remove that curse in my own marriage? Perhaps. Whatever... I'd chosen to look for a leader in a husband.

Is Steve the one? I wondered as we walked hand in hand toward 24 Flavors.

When we arrived, Steve ordered.

"A cherry milkshake for my girl," he said without even asking me what I wanted.

Hmm, I thought. I liked having a strong man take charge of my smallest want.

⁓

The next Saturday night was Gonzaga Prom. Steve arrived at Marian Hall (this time he didn't *assume*—he'd asked) with a gorgeous orchid. (It was my first-ever orchid—I was impressed!)

I wore an aqua net and taffeta ballerina strapless formal.

We were double-dating with Steve's friend Dirks and his date Pat. Any worries I had about going to Prom with an "older man" (Steve was already 21) were quelled. Pat had gone to Glasgow High School—she'd been a senior when I was a sophomore—a *nice girl* my mother said.

Dirks had the car—he drove. Steve and I got better acquainted in the back seat.

Minutes after we left Marian Hall, Dirks stopped. I looked out expecting to see a big building—The Spokane Club—the prom site.

I saw a big building all right—but the flashing sign in front said *Carlton Hotel*.

Oh my gosh! I thought. *What have I gotten myself into?*

I looked at Pat. She smiled at me, as if everything was normal.

We all got out, entered the lobby, got into the elevator. My heart was beating a mile a minute.

I started saying Hail Marys. Silently.

Now I can't say my mother had warned me not to go to hotels with dates. "Be a good girl" had been the extent of my sex education at home.

But I knew what *could* happen. There'd been an instance in Glasgow where a local girl and her sixteen-year-old *customer* were arrested at the Roosevelt Hotel. She was sent to the Montana State Girl's Reformatory, and the guy ended up in the Boy's Reformatory in Miles City. They hadn't been playing tiddlywinks.

We heard music and lots of voices as we exited the elevator. Dirks and Pat walked down the hall like they were going to English class. Entered a room and disappeared.

Thank goodness it wasn't the first time I'd worn three-inch heels. I'm sure my knees were shaking.

Steve waited at the door like the gentleman he was and motioned me inside.

With one last check as to how many doors the elevator was from where I was entering—ready for a quick getaway—I swallowed. Took a right.

"It's about time," said a friend of Steve I'd met before but couldn't name. "I pour the first drink, but after that you're on your own."

The room was filled with couples talking and drinking and having fun.

(I never told Steve until after we were married how scared I'd been by my experience at the Carleton Hotel. He was amazed. The guys always rented a hotel room for a before-prom party—it was standard procedure.)

About an hour later we ended up at the real destination—The Spokane Club.

We danced and danced and danced. I floated in his arms.

A week later—Holy Names Prom—wearing another orchid on my wrist, Steve guided me through the French doors of the Spokane Country Club. We danced under the stars. I felt like Ginger Rogers—Steve was Fred Astaire.

The next Saturday, we went to downtown Spokane to watch the Lilac Parade. I'd never seen such a sight before—float after float of flowers and pretty girls dressed in shades of lavender. Dozens of bands.

Afterwards, we met Steve's cousin Nick and his wife Virginia. They treated us to a hamburger lunch at Knight's Diner.

Chapter 1

Darlene and Steve at Gonzaga Prom three weeks after their first date

Sunday was Mother's Day. Steve and I joined Jerry and Midge. In a rented motorboat, we swished back and forth on Hayden Lake in nearby Idaho.

"There's Bing Crosby's cabin," Jerry said.

Some cabin, I thought. *It looks like more like a mansion to me.*

Steve entertained us with stories about Mrs. Lemmon—who cooked at Holy Names College for the nuns and students during the school year and for Bing at his summer place every June, July, and August. She spoiled Steve and Jerry serving them the special food the nuns ate in the kitchen while the girls in the dining room ate regular.

After stopping the boat at a deserted dock, the guys tied up the boat, and we two couples parted on the shore.

It was May. Romantic...

Almost dark by the time we got back, Jerry let Steve and me off at the corner of Boone and Superior. We took the long way home. Through Mission Park.

I wasn't expecting what happened next. Hadn't an inkling. Not a hint.

With just three weeks since our first dance, our first date... With only a score or so of kisses—exciting but chaste... With me not-quite-nineteen and Steve just-turned-twenty-one... He asked, "Will you marry me?"

In shock, I didn't answer immediately. Not "Yes." Not "No."

The next three weeks are a blur. I only I remember three things for sure from that time: It never rained; Steve and I spent every single spare minute together; I got an A+ on my term paper.

Then I said "Yes."

After a whirlwind of changed plans, I got into the back seat of Steve's friend Marty's car and headed to Butte, Montana to meet the parents of my new fiancé.

My eyes were closed. I felt the circular motion of his finger on my palm, the pressure of his touch, the heat of his lips on mine.

I was floating in the backseat of a '50 Studebaker. In ecstasy, I opened my eyes. Surfaced to hear him say, "There's Butte," as Marty drove down the hill and Highway 10 wound toward what has been called "The Richest Hill on Earth."

As we approached the city that May evening in 1955, it felt as if we were on a space-ship ducking through the Northern Lights on our way to a rendezvous on Earth.

"You never told me Butte is beautiful," I chastised him.

"I didn't know," he confided.

He kissed me quiet.

That night I slept in a house on Grand Avenue, in a double bed, crammed between my friend Colleen and her *soon-to-be niece*. I dreamed of wearing

Chapter 1

a white satin wedding dress, saying, "I do," kissing Steve on the altar of St. Raphael's Church in front of God and everyone.

The next morning he arrived in his parent's car and drove me up the Hill.

Having lived on the prairie of eastern Montana for eighteen years, I thought I'd seen barren hills. I knew at that moment, I'd no idea what *barren* meant before. The Great Plains had not prepared me for the *nothingness*. As Steve gave me a guided tour through the once thriving metropolis, I saw what the locals apparently didn't—Butte was dying.

I kept my discovery to myself. Steve seemed to love his hometown.

He drove up Arizona Street, turned slightly to the right on the Anaconda Road, and then took a quick left into what seemed to be a dirt field. An ancient log cabin, sod roof and all, stood on the left. He took a quick right and said, "Here we are."

My intended—the epitome of the fifties Big Man on Campus, who'd just been elected Senior Class President of a prestigious university—had stopped in the middle of a slum and said, "We're home."

Right then and there, I thought, *Wow! I've made the right choice. Steve's come so far in twenty-one years—on his own. He's a real keeper*!

I was not prepared for Butte. The Flats were a lot like Glasgow, Montana where I grew up—old houses mixed up with a few built after WWII. Nothing fancy, just houses.

My guide to see *The Richest Hill on Earth* showed me the town. "There's Meaderville over that way." Steve waved toward the right. "We'll have to go eat at Lydia's. It's a legend. My cousin George used to have a place down there too—the Savoy."

Approaching downtown, we saw a couple of big holes between buildings. "Just another fire," Steve said. "They call it urban renewal," he laughed—a hollow laugh.

It seemed to me that every other sign advertised a bar. We parked the car and began walking. I was shocked to see drunks staggering from one watering hole to another—at 9 a.m.

Later, as we drove down Park headed out of downtown Butte, Steve said, "Gotta show you the West Side."

The first *site*—and I italicize that because at that moment in my life it was the most beautiful house I'd ever seen—was the mansion of Copper

King Marcus Daly. With four two-story white columns holding up the third floor balcony, it reminded me of what Scarlet's Tara must have looked like. (I'd never even seen the movie—just read *Gone with the Wind*.)

There were two others I'd categorize as mansions—one had belonged to a second Copper King, William Clark, and the third to his son Charles. But there were scores of stately two and three story homes on streets named Gold, Platinum, Silver, and Quartz.

Steve turned down Diamond Street and said, "There's the house where my special girlfriend in high school lived—her dad was a lawyer for the ACM." He explained that the ACM—Anaconda Copper Mining—owned every mine on the Butte Hill. "One way or another, the ACM owns this town and everyone in it."

In awe I looked at my new fiancé and realized another facet of his life.

At dinner that night, Steve's father said, "Ya show her the West Side?"

Steve nodded.

"Just so you know what Butte's really like, that's where the Rich Bitches live," Steve's father said, a sneer on his face.

I saw Steve cringe.

Over the years, I learned to treasure Butte, a city where I found no one is judged by *where* they live, but only *how* they live. I've often said—and Steve agrees—that I understand Butte better than most natives.

During the week I stayed in Butte, Steve kept me busy meeting relatives. His folks were welcoming. Cautiously.

The first thing his sister, Sis, said was, "Those sure are funny yellow shoes." Then she asked, "When are you leaving?" *Oh, oh,* I thought.

But I immediately fell in love with Steve's nine-year-old sister Dorothy Jean—or *Dodo,* her nickname. I bonded with Dodo as I watched her play dolls with two little friends, Marie and Mary Jo. The nine year age gap made no difference—she was my sister.

Steve introduced me to dozens of relatives (his father had eleven siblings, his mother three).

He took me to The Gardens where we rode the (mini-sized, thank goodness) roller coaster and had ice cream. Together, we dreamed about

Chapter 1

the old days when the Big Bands played dances at the pavilion. Tommy Dorsey, Harry James, Billy May—Steve had danced to them all.

We went swimming at Gregson.

I wanted to see a mine, so he took me to the Kelley. What a disappointment! We rode an elevator down to a cavern paved in green concrete. Even then I dreamed about walking in mine tunnels dug by pickax or blown by dynamite.

But I'm getting ahead of my story.

〜

That July, Steve rode the bus up to Glasgow with a diamond ring that he proudly put on my finger.

We were officially engaged!

With Steve working in Butte that summer my social life disappeared. We saw each other a total of five days June through August.

Then—in September—Steve got the chance to prove his love.

In late August a bee stung me on my nose resulting in what my doctor called a *classic case* of HSV-Type 1 (an orofacial disease commonly called a cold sore). I hadn't gone to the doctor immediately when the tiny pustules began appearing—my father was a big believer in home remedies. By the time I went to see Dr. Smith, the lower third of my nose and face looked like an open sore.

When I got off the Empire Builder in Spokane that September, strangers were asking me about *the terrible accident* I'd been in. I was one big scab.

Steve took one look at me, said, "You weren't kidding—you look terrible." And he gave me a big kiss like nothing was different.

Oh how I loved that man! Most guys would have asked for their ring back and run the other way at full speed. I had a winner!

College that year was perfect. As Senior Class President Steve had free tickets for everything. Mixers every Friday night, basketball games, concerts, plays, a movie at the COG (student union) every Sunday (if we weren't doing something more exciting—which we often were). We saw each other every day.

Then there were the big things—The Military Ball, Valentine Gala, Gonzaga Prom, Holy Names Prom.

Steve bought me so many cherry milkshakes at Johnson's 24 Flavors that the owners of the ice cream shop probably had to lower their income estimates after we left school.

But . . . Now is probably as good a place as any to discuss Steve's net worth—$0.

I knew he paid his tuition by working in the Butte mines during the summer and delivering mail for the post office at Christmas. That he earned his board and room janitoring at Holy Names. I was really proud of his ambition.

Money was a challenge for him—after buying my ring with most of his summer earnings, Steve still had to finance his 1955-56 tuition and our *fun* money. So, besides carrying a full load, doing his class president duties, and seeing me, he got two additional cleaning jobs—at Johnson's 24 Flavors and Drs. Wendell and Nishimura's medical office. When he slept, I'll never know.

What I *do* know is—he treated me like a queen. I doubt a king could have shown his bride-to-be a better time.

In the spring two miracles happened.

My folks sold some property and chose to buy us a car as a wedding present. *Wow!*

Steve hadn't even had a jalopy. His folks didn't own a car until he was a junior in high school.

We basked in our luck.

And . . . We got a house.

At that time we had no idea houses would become our *thing*. We still chuckle at how much we loved the tiny model home we toured during one of our first dates.

That spring, as we were planning our wedding, we started looking for a place to live. It didn't take us long to discover—houses were expensive. One realtor actually said, "You two have no potential." (We fooled him! Eventually.)

But one house builder, after finding we couldn't afford the down payment for his beautiful new home in the Spokane Valley, offered us a deal.

"I've got a two bedroom house I'd like to sell you. Just got it on trade. Six-hundred square feet. Just a block from the Spokane River. Three hundred dollars down and $60 a month."

We checked it out. Without any furniture—and with stars in our eyes—it looked like a palace. It had those aqua steel kitchen cabinets I'd

Chapter 1

loved in the model home, a wood-burning fireplace in the living room, and a full, unfinished basement with another brick fireplace.

The kitchen and bathroom were painted the brightest shade of orange I've ever seen—like they were the background of two Gaugin frescos. The living room was a vibrant, dark aqua. The master bedroom glowed—chartreuse on the ceiling and shocking pink walls. The second bedroom was all chartreuse.

"I couldn't sleep here," I moaned.

"Don't think I could do *anything* in this bedroom," Steve said suggestively.

I blushed.

"Don't worry," he said. "I know how to use a paintbrush."

We agreed to paint the bedrooms the first day we got back from our honeymoon.

Yes, we were hooked.

Steve negotiated.

"Save it for us 'til August 26? Wait for the down payment 'til then? First payment on September 1?"

We owned our first home. (Well, almost.)

That summer Steve worked overtime in the Butte mines. As usual, I managed the laundry in my folk's motel in Glasgow. It was lonely—except for the week before the Fourth of July.

My parents had sold fireworks just outside the city limits since I was in sixth grade. In 1956 they said, "Would you like to share the stand with us this summer? We'll supply the store and the merchandise. You and Steve do the work. We'll split the profits—half and half."

Sounded great to us.

And it was. When we sold the last firecracker, Steve and I divided the silver dollars with my folks and headed for the store. By the time we were done we'd bought a refrigerator, a kitchen table and four chairs, a sofa bed, a rocker, a folding bed, and had a couple of hundred dollars left for our honeymoon. With our shower presents, wedding gifts, and my bedroom set, cedar chest, cabinet-type sewing machine (that looked like a credenza), we were set.

I've loved fireworks ever since!

Chapter 2

STEVE ALMOST ARRIVED IN Glasgow too late—we hadn't realized the required blood tests took time to process. Thank goodness for dear Dr. Smith who used his clout to speed things along.

Father Altmann gave Steve and me our wedding instructions—an hour of information about the new rectory the parish was building—and this suggestion for Steve—"Don't keep her barefoot and pregnant." He didn't have any words of wisdom for me. *Hmm*!

At 9 a.m., on Saturday, August 18, 1956, we were married at St. Raphael's Church. I promised to "love and cherish" Steve forever. "For better or worse, for richer or poorer, in sickness and in health, until death do we part."

I've never admitted this before, but I don't remember *what* Steve promised. It must have pleased our priest though as I did hear him say, "I now pronounce you man and wife."

The reception was a professionally decorated cake—thanks to Steve's chef uncle, Nick Cladis—coffee, tea, and assorted mints. And a lunch catered by The Altar Society ladies for everyone—courtesy of my parents.

(We heard later that Steve's father questioned if the wedding was even legal.)

"Where's the booze?" he'd complained. "It's not a marriage without booze!"

Apparently he stopped by the liquor store on his way back to the motel—loaded up with sufficient spirits to float a battleship. He hosted his own affair. (My parents weren't invited, although they'd provided the whole wedding party with free rooms.)

We left about 1:00 p.m. in a car that Steve's devious friends had defaced with slogans like *Sucker, Does your mother know*? And worse.

Chapter 2

Not quite halfway to our destination of Havre (150 miles from Glasgow), just outside of Malta, we encountered a road block. Two sheriff's cars had totally stopped traffic on the two-lane highway.

Getting out slowly, one sheriff approached. Motioned for Steve to roll down his window.

"Keep your hands on the wheel, young man. Got a call this car's been stolen."

"Damned Marty!" Steve grumbled.

Oh my God! I thought. *I'm going to spend my wedding night in jail.*

Steve sat behind the wheel in his brand-new, navy blue suit. I'd changed from my silk gown with a long train to a short white sheath. My gloves were off, but I still wore a white hat.

Luckily the officer saw the signage on our car—and put two and two together. Laughing he said, "Hope I haven't slowed you kids up too long."

We were off in five minutes.

Steve drove. Fast.

I kept him company reading excerpts from a wedding present (given to my new husband by his married friend, John—the one who he'd chosen over me that first night), a thin paperback entitled *The Marriage Night*.

We got our money's worth from the Ranch Motel before dinner time. Then we took a break, donned regular clothes, walked down to the big hotel on Main Street, and had hamburgers and milkshakes.

Afterwards was a bonus.

We did have a snafu when we finally opened our suitcases. Wheat rolled out of Steve's—rice from mine (and rolled and continued to roll out, a grain or two at a time, for years). Someone had sewed the bottoms of my nightgowns shut. Luckily, I had a manicure scissors in my cosmetic bag. Glad we hadn't waited to enjoy our wedded state before we got ready to sleep that evening, we went to bed for the umpteenth time that Saturday, our wedding day.

We'd been married thirty days. It was Sunday. After church. After a late breakfast (no one called it brunch then). We'd just gotten *comfy*. In bed.

Someone knocked at the front door. Once. Twice.

Steve jumped up. Peeked out a corner of the draw drape. (The window was directly next to the front porch.)

"My God! It's Helen and Bob," he said—sotto voce.

Now Helen had been my best friend at college—Steve went to Gonzaga with Bob. They were engaged. Not married. I'd invited Helen to *drop by sometime.*

We both stopped breathing.

After what seemed like eons, we heard a car engine rev up.

We breathed a sigh of relief. Began where we'd left off.

Funny thing—after that Helen and Bob always called before they *dropped by.*

We'd been back from our week-long honeymoon to Glacier for 37 days. And I was *late.*

At the recommendation of Margie, my married friend, I made an appointment with Dr. Rotchford, an OB/GYN.

"You're pregnant," he said. "Barely."

I guess barely. We'd followed the rules until August 18, our wedding day. How did this happen?

Through a fog of unbelief, I heard the doctor say, "I'd like your husband to come to your next appointment."

A couple of weeks later, I sat in the doctor's waiting room while the nurse took Steve aside. "To take a blood sample," she said.

After pleasantries, the doctor said, "The two of you have a challenge. Your blood doesn't match. Maybe someday it won't be a problem, but in 1956, this is serious."

"Serious? What are you talking about?" we both cried.

"You've heard of blue babies I'm sure," he said.

I remembered when movie star Lana Turner's "blue" baby almost died before it had a total blood change.

"Could our baby die?" I gasped.

"That's why we're looking at your pregnancy. Darlene, you have O negative blood. Steve has AB positive. That means your RH factors are fighting with each other in the baby who's growing in Darlene's womb."

We were stunned. We hadn't even *planned* on being pregnant at this point in our infant marriage. We were supposed to be having fun.

Dr. Rotchford explained. "First babies are the easiest. Often you make it through that one with no problem. But we can't take a chance. Darlene, I want you in my office for blood titers every month for the first four months. Twice a month after January and weekly after April 1. Until your due date of

CHAPTER 2

June 3. But don't plan on making it to term. In fact, having this baby early will give it a better chance."

Then the doctor dropped the bombshell. "I have to tell you right off, the two of you shouldn't have a lot of babies. And—definitely—you shouldn't have them one after the other."

My God! Didn't he realize we hadn't even been married two months? Didn't he know we were Catholic? Didn't he know how you made babies?

We were in the middle of our first storm.

Time passed. We lived. We loved.

I got a job—$200 a month. Steve began his *Fifth Year*—an accelerated program for an Education Degree. And got a part-time job—at Wes's Phillips gas station at the corner of Boone and Hamilton. (We still had tuition to pay.)

Buying our groceries, I followed my college home economics teacher's budget for two adults—$15 a week. We feasted on homemade pizza (a box of Chef Boyardee and a half-pound of hamburger—25 cents for the meat). And ate Dinty Moore stew—warmed—right out of the can. One week I splurged on a pork roast—but saved it in the fridge too long. It smelled rotten when I took it out of the plastic. I sobbed—it was supposed to feed us for two nights—and sandwiches.

My folks came to check on us in late October. My mother was *not* happy over my pregnancy.

"You just got married," she whined. "What will people say? For heaven's sake, don't have *it* too soon!"

Furious, I thought, *Like I can stop what's already in process?*

Steve and I really lucked out with our first neighbors—the McGraths—Clara and Bart. In their mid-forties, we had nothing in common.

They rented the house next door in early September and almost immediately invited us for dinner. Barbecued hamburgers the first night. They were the best we'd ever eaten, and we told them so. Clara and Bart beamed.

Next Bart cooked two-inch-thick pork chops on their outdoor barbecue, and Clara made corn on the cob. I'd never had my fill of that delight before in my life. My mother cooked three cobs of corn, one for my father, one for her, and one for me. That was it. Clara cooked enough for an army that night. (Found out she'd been an Army nurse during WWII.) She kept asking me if I wanted more—I kept accepting.

When we got home, Steve said, "I don't want to make you feel bad, but do you have any idea how many cobs of corn you ate?"

I looked blank. I'd been too busy eating to count.

"Seven!" he said. "I've got to tell you, Darlene, if Clara hadn't been so sweet about it, I'd have been embarrassed."

My appetite couldn't have scared the McGraths off. They soon invited us over for spaghetti and meatballs. Absolutely delicious!

Steve told them about my culinary attempt at Italian food—"Chef Boyardee out of a can. Not a meatball in sight."

I explained, "That's what my mother cooked—I have no idea how to make the real thing. In fact I'd never even *tasted* real Italian spaghetti until Steve took me to Lydia's in Butte."

"Would you like me to teach you how to make my Sicilian grandmother's recipe?" Clara offered.

I jumped at the chance.

"Do you have a big pot?" she asked. "A grater? An electric fry pan?"

I nodded. We'd gotten lots of kitchen gadgets for shower and wedding presents.

Clara wrote out my grocery list. "That's it, except the cheese. I get a big block of a special Romano at Tito's once a month. I'll share enough for your first batch."

The next Saturday morning Clara arrived at 9 a.m., and the two of us got to work in our dollhouse-sized kitchen. (It was so handy you could stand in the middle of the room, cook at the stove, set the table, and wash dishes in the sink without moving more than a couple of feet in any direction.)

"Open the puree first," Clara directed. "Next, add the tomato paste. Fill one empty puree can with warm water, swish it around, and add to the mixture. Then peel a clove of garlic and put it—whole—into the sauce in the pan."

I must say, as I peeled that garlic I was glad my mother wasn't there. She'd have been horrified. "Only poor people eat garlic!" she told me in no uncertain terms when my home economics teacher in ninth grade cooking class recommended halving a clove of garlic, squeezing it gently, and rubbing it on the entire inside of the salad bowl.

"Never in *my* house," my mother said in her *I'm-the-boss-and-you-better-know-it* voice.

Chapter 2

Finally, Clara had me put a handful of commercial parmesan cheese in the tomato mixture. "Turn the burner on low and let it cook.

"Now it's time to make meatballs."

At Clara's direction, I got out my biggest Pyrex bowl, the yellow one. She had me put in the two-pound package of hamburger I'd gotten at the IGA grocery store, two slices of grated white bread, and one whole egg.

"Now grate the Romano cheese."

I almost died as she handed me the round ball. *The cheese was green*!

Clara saw me flinch—and explained, "Just the rind is green. Cut off a chunk. Grate the white part and put into our mixture."

Finally there were only three unused bottles on the counter. One filled with dark green flakes, another with medium, and a third labeled powered garlic. (I'd have to hide *that* at Christmas time when my mother came to visit.)

Clara proceeded to teach me how to *smidge*. Fingers were used instead of measuring spoons. She demonstrated on a piece of wax paper. Had me practice a few times. "You're a natural smidger, Darlene," she said.

"Now—two smidges each of the sweet basil and oregano. One of garlic powder."

Then we *hand-mashed* the meat/herb combination, tweaked out enough for individual meatballs, rolled the meat in balls, and browned each sphere in oil. That finished, we slid them into the tomato mixture on the stove.

"You're done. Great job, Darlene. Stir every fifteen minutes. Simmer all day (it was only 11 a.m.). Follow the directions on the package of spaghetti, make a little salad, and you've got a meal."

Right then I decided, *I'm going to take a fresh clove of garlic tonight, slice it down the middle, squeeze it good and hard, and roll it around the entire inside of my salad bowl.*

As she was getting ready to leave, Clara produced a loaf of French bread and said, "Bart got this for you and Steve. Enjoy."

As she was leaving, Clara said, "Remember, next Saturday night I'm making veal and peppers. Come about five, and we'll have a glass of wine."

Minutes later—standing alone in my kitchen, I had the most amazing thought. *Why, I've just been given Clara's family-secret spaghetti recipe.*

It was hard to believe—here was Clara, an almost-complete-stranger from Troy, New York—treating me like her own daughter.

I felt very special.

Thanksgiving loomed. We only had enough money to buy hotdogs. "They'll be fun cooked over the flames in our own fireplace," I encouraged my husband who longed for turkey.

The Saturday before the holiday, John and Margie invited us up to their place. When we arrived, we found the plan was for John and Steve to go to the St. Charles annual bazaar. Margie and I were going to stay home with the kids and make cookies.

I wasn't prepared for the whooping and hollering three hours later. Steve came in waving a five dollar bill. John followed saying, "Look what else Steve won." It was a 25 pound turkey. *Happy* is an understatement.

We ate turkey for ten days. I swear. Thursday was just us. I cooked the gravy—my very first attempt. It didn't thicken. I poured in more flour. More. Got dumplings. It was wonderful!

Friday was a no meat day—pre-Vatican II. Saturday we invited John, Margie, and their three kids over for leftovers. We pulled our kitchen table into the living room. Lifted up the two leaves (we couldn't fit the expanded version in our tiny kitchen). We had lots of food (thanks to that extra five dollars). Had lots of laughs.

Steve took a picture of the whole Donoghue family, John, Margie, Mary Kaye, Jimmie John, and Mark—with me sitting in the middle.

Jimmie John looked the situation over and asked in his three-year-old logic, "How come you don't have a TV? What do you sit and watch?" (We bought one—on payments—immediately after.)

The next Monday, my childhood friend Gail arrived. We ate turkey. Had a wonderful reunion. Although not related, I considered him my twin brother. I'd cried when the Navy hadn't allowed him a furlough to come home for my wedding.

Steve and I continued eating turkey until it was rancid. He never got sick. I did. He said it was because I was pregnant. (Note: it was a good forty years before I really enjoyed eating turkey again. *Hmm!*)

Even then, Christmas was my favorite holiday of the year. Both Steve and I had grown up in homes where there were only two decorations: a three-foot Christmas tree sitting on top of our mother's sewing machine and two

Chapter 2

red cellophane wreaths, each with an electric candle in the center, placed in the middle of our frosted-over front windows.

The second Sunday that first December we drove over to Idaho, getting wet in snow up to our armpits in our search of the perfect spruce. We came home with our hand-cut tree—a tree Steve had to supplement by drilling holes with a brace and bit and inserting extra branches. Perfect? Maybe not—but beautiful to us.

A dozen glass ornaments, a string of multi-colored lights, and a couple of boxes of aluminum icicles—each strand painstakingly put on separately—decorated the evergreen we'd gone to such efforts to obtain.

Five plaster-of-Paris choirboys, each three inches high—just purchased at Sears, held the place of honor in the center of our mantle. (After sixty Christmases, we still have two of those keepsakes—displayed in a special place yearly. Our daughter Stephanie hangs the remaining colored balls on her tree.)

It was almost Christmas—our very first Christmas together. Snow fell outside—big, saucer-like flakes.

Steve made a fire with wood we'd scavengered in our Christmas-tree-cutting Sunday. Neither of us had ever lived in a home with a fireplace. We soaked up the warmth, the ambiance.

"Let's go for a walk so we can see the smoke come out of our chimney," he suggested.

The beauty of the night was breathtaking. Our love surrounded us like a warm blanket as we stood a block away, watching the smoke curlicue from our chimney. Holding hands through mittens on the way back was as sensuous as our first intimate touch.

"I'll never forget tonight," I predicted. He agreed. We never did.

By the first of May, I'd gained fifteen pounds, was being titered every week, and had just worked my last day at Tel Electric. (I felt great. But my boss seemed a bit nervous having an eight-month pregnant woman walking up to the second floor every day.)

I had two projects planned for the week—spring cleaning and typing Steve's term paper. A chemistry major—my husband's dissertation was way over my head. (Years later I discovered it was a 1956 explanation of DNA testing. No wonder—with only two semesters of college chemistry under my belt—I'd thought it was Greek.)

My girlfriends gave me a baby shower on May 8. After they left, I got down on my hands and knees and scrubbed the floors. (In retrospect, I doubt they were very dirty, but those were my Mrs. Clean days.)

During the night, I started having pains in my back. They progressed to my tummy. Steve called the doctor who said, "Bring her in."

When we got to the hospital and parked, the pains stopped. I refused to go in.

"Margie said they'd charge us for a whole day if I get admitted, my labor stops, and I get sent home." Given our money situation, we decided to walk around the Spokane reservoir and see what happened.

It was a glorious, sunny May morning. I had my hand in Steve's pocket—keeping as close to him as possible.

The pains came and went. At 6:30 a.m. I grunted. Grabbed him so hard, I split his pants six inches down his leg.

"I don't care *what* they charge us," Steve said. "I'm not staying out here with you in this condition a minute more!"

In five hours, we had a beautiful daughter—Catherine Michele.

But, three days later—when Steve came to check us out—he had a major problem. We'd gotten a $150 refund from our income tax—and used it to pay the doctor. Now the hospital wanted $100.55. Steve's teaching job (he'd gotten lucky and been hired at Otis Orchards High School in the Spokane Valley so we could stay in our house) wouldn't start until September. He needed a summer job. We barely had enough money saved to buy groceries for the month.

"I can't pay you now," he said.

"That's not acceptable, Mr. Matule."

"You can't get money out of a turnip," he explained.

"Well! I never! Rules are rules. You can't take your wife and baby home until the bill is paid. In full."

"I'll have it taken care of by the first of September."

"Unacceptable."

"Okay," he said as he turned to leave. "I'll be back to pick them up when I've got all the money. The hospital can give them board and room 'til then." He began walking away.

"Now, Mr. Matule," he heard. He continued toward the door.

"Mr. Matule. Come back. We'll work something out."

A half hour later, the three of us were driving north to our home on Montgomery Street.

Chapter 2

By late August, paying $10 a week (Steve had gotten a job at Allied Truck Lines in June), I wrote the final check to Sacred Heart Hospital. We celebrated with milkshakes from The Westminster on Division Street.

⤳

Ten days later, on May 21, I celebrated my twenty-first birthday. Virtually all by myself.

Steve was at class during the day. In the evening he went to a big Gonzaga shindig at the Ridpath Hotel. Although I was invited (it was one of those free things—Steve was Vice President of the Student Body that year), things had changed. My baby daughter needed me.

My mother had come on the train to help after Michele was born. But . . . She'd forgotten everything she ever knew about taking care of an infant. She couldn't even manage the brand new automatic washer and dryer we'd bought on time. Even though the doctor said "no stairs for a month," I still had to walk up and down daily—albeit slowly—to do the laundry. She *did* cook—but baking was my mother's thing, not cooking.

I decided to have a little pity party. All by myself.

Where was my fun? Why wasn't I dancing at the Ridpath? Why wasn't I eating steak and lobster? Why wasn't I enjoying a celebratory glass of champagne? You only turn twenty-one once! I told myself.

I remembered the school year of 1955-56—the year Steve and I were engaged. One fun thing after another.

As they said in the movies, *Ain't love grand?* Steve and I had watched Grace Kelly and Bing Crosby in *High Society* on our honeymoon. I could see Steve and me on that yacht, singing *True Love*. I could see myself in Grace's gorgeous gowns (some of the dresses I sewed with my own two hands were equally lovely if I do say so myself.) I'd worn those gowns. I'd danced at the best hotels, the finest country clubs. Dined at the Manito Country Club with a Gonzaga supporter—I'd enjoyed my first raw oysters that evening. At my wedding I'd worn a bridal dress that had been featured on the *Modern Bride* cover.

Oh, I'd been spoiled! And I'd taken it all for granted!

The baby cried. I took her in my arms, calmed her. I gazed at the perfection that Steve and I had unknowingly created while we were enjoying the beauty of our love. Her little fingernails were just forming. She clutched my thumb.

I knew right then. Life is a miracle. With ups—and downs. I was where I was meant to be. Doing what I was meant to do.

I heard the car in the driveway. Met Steve at the back door. Together we hurried to our bedroom. Made sure the latch was closed tight (my mother was sleeping across the hall). Lay beside each other and cuddled.

I celebrated the last moments of the perfect twenty-first birthday—in my love's arms, my baby daughter two steps away.

God is good!

In the next three years I learned many things.

Daily discomfort—when I took my temperature, rectally, every morning before I got out of the bed, to see if I was ovulating.

Frustration—his and mine—as I had to say, once again, "Not tonight."

Acceptance as we spent our first wedding anniversary eating a take-out pizza. Watching Debby Reynolds in *Tammy* at the drive-in movie theatre—with Michele in her detached buggy in the back seat. (I still remember every detail whenever I hear anyone sing, "Tammy, Tammy, Tammy's in love.")

Toasting our first year together—after the movie—with root beers in the A&W parking lot.

Happiness when, after a year and a half, we moved to a bigger house. We still had the aqua blue cabinets. But we'd acquired a dining room "el"—we could leave the two leaves of our table up all the time. And it had three bedrooms—master, Michele's nursery, and an extra bedroom. Plus a bigger monthly house payment—$15 more. I quickly learned how much $15 could be.

Shock as Michele stopped breathing—a hard candy lodged in her throat. But Steve knew just what to do. He banged her tiny chest. Turned her upside down. Willed the round sphere out her mouth.

Joy as she sputtered, reached for me, and said, "Mommy."

Worry as Steve began having bouts of intense pain—and blood in his urine.

Horror when we heard the news—kidney stones. How could this be? He'd just turned 24. We had no hospital insurance (couldn't afford it).

Desperation as the surgeon said, "This is an emergency. Steve will *die* if he doesn't have surgery. Right now!"

Exhaustion as I worked at my new job in the bowels of the Old National Bank—a job taken to pay off the bill for the surgeon and Steve's two-week

Chapter 2

stay at the hospital. Daily I worked eight hours, visited Steve, got Michele from the babysitter, and did whatever was needed at home.

And—the next day—began all over again.

***

During that time, I remember thinking. *This isn't what I signed up for. It's not fair!*

I'd expected good stuff in my marriage. Sure, I'd said the, "better or worse, richer or poorer, in sickness or in health" words at our wedding.

But I'd never given a thought to the *worse*, or *poorer*, or *sickness* parts *actually happening*. Not to us!

Looking back, I think I needed a taste of humility.

In the meantime, Steve went through the indignities of post op.

I remember the first night. As we visited, a feeble-looking old man kept walking back and forth in front of Steve's open door. The oldster wore a knee-length, gaping-in-the-back hospital gown—he towed a bag of gurgling liquid on rollers.

"There's no way I'll ever be hooked to one of those things!" my young, strong husband bragged.

The next night, and thirteen more after that, I walked up and down the hall with Steve as he towed a similar appendage. However, at the suggestion of one of the nurses who Steve had known at Gonzaga, I'd brought his bathrobe so his backside was covered.

In retrospect, I believe that summer was good for us. And for our marriage.

We learned we could go to the depths—Steve had been at the edge of death. Yet he'd not just come back, he'd fought his way forward.

I'd planted some Shasta daisy seeds beside our house that spring. The soil was sandy. I'd not fertilized. But they popped out of the ground as happy as if I'd given them a daily drink of Miracle Grow.

"Flower," I said to our fourteen-month daughter, pointing to the blooming plant.

Her eyes lit up. With perfect diction, Michele said, "Flow—er. Flow—er. Flow—er." She pursed her lips on the second syllable as if she were puckering up for a kiss. And she giggled.

Steve and I never looked back.

Within a week, he was back at his summer job working for the Spokane Park Department.

Immediately, we got hospital insurance. We might not be able to afford it, but we realized we couldn't afford to be without.

I continued working, moved from sorting checks to computer entry, to being a teller. It wasn't my dream job, but my parents now lived in Spokane. For $100 a month they babysat. I paid off Steve's hospital bill. We started saving money.

On August 18 we celebrated our second anniversary with dinner at the Ridpath Hotel (main floor King Cole Room, not the view *Top*.). We felt blessed.

We began planning our *dream* home. On Sunday afternoons we toured open houses.

Within walking distance of our church and a new elementary school, we found a neighborhood we loved. We made friends with a contractor who built beautiful houses. We drooled.

And then—by a fluke (the builder had an "open house" that didn't sell)—he offered to take our little three bedroom project house as most of the down payment. The catch? Steve had to work as an assistant carpenter that summer on the builder's jobs-in-process.

We jumped at the opportunity.

Chapter 3

"It's a dream come true," I gushed as I walked through our new, custom, three bedroom, two bath, brick home. I could open both leaves of our original table in the kitchen. Besides, we had a separate dining room where a brand new dining room table and six chairs sat waiting for our first guests. Our one car looked lonely in the attached two-car garage. But—it gave us lots of room for *stuff*.

After our sweat labor, we had a 2,400 square-foot home with a full basement that featured a huge family room, large laundry, fourth bedroom/study, and ample storage space where Steve constructed custom shelves for our pantry items. Plus a covered patio in our fenced back yard.

Before I continue my memoir, I have to explain how my parents became a daily part of the Matule story.

When Michele was ten months old, they sold their motel in Glasgow and bought a house in Spokane—two doors from us. A few months after Steve and I moved into our Cascade Way home, they followed us—got a place one house east of ours.

Conflict ensued.

If we had a neighborhood girl babysit—my mother complained. If we asked her to take care of Michele and Stephanie while Steve and I went out, my mother fussed. I couldn't win.

My mother had a habit of coming to *visit*—uninvited—five minutes after a car full of company parked in front of our house. She drove me crazy.

My daddy was a saint.

We lived with our unique problem. Sometimes it worked better than others.

Sixty Shades of Love

Steve's sister Dodo came for the first summer—she'd jumped at the chance to be our babysitter and avoid the tension of troubles at home in Butte.

We'd just finished paying the bill for Steve's kidney surgery, but had decided that I should keep working at the Old National Bank so we could buy some extras for our new house.

Steve planted our front lawn on the Fourth of July. We bought a swing set that took up the left corner of our backyard. The rest we kept natural (which meant he mowed the weeds). That left an area in front of the kitchen and dining room empty.

"We need a few bushes," Steve said. "Some white rocks to set them off."

"Bushes are *not* in the budget!" I said. (I watched our money down to the penny.)

A heated discussion followed. A *very* heated discussion!

The next Saturday, while Dodo, Michele, and I were getting ready for an outing with Steve, he disappeared.

When he came home with five evergreen bushes and four bags of white rock, I yelled, "What did you use for money?" I knew he had no cash and didn't carry checks.

"No problem. The nursery took that new credit card we just got."

"The one we were going to use *only* for emergencies?" I gasped.

I have no idea what else I said. But after all these years, Steve still remembers how our fighting got so bad it upset his sister. So, even though our family was in chaos, he loaded all of us in the car—he needed a file from his office. By the time we were in downtown Spokane, Dodo was gagging in the back seat—about to throw up.

"Steve, Dodo needs a bathroom," I said. "Fast!"

As Steve drove by The Crescent, he saw a loading zone. Desperate, he parked—even though he could have gotten a big ticket.

The minute the car stopped, I got Dodo out of the back seat and rushed her to the nearest bathroom. We barely made it.

Neither Dodo nor Michele remember the event. But it was pivotal in our marriage.

We learned a big lesson that day—you never buy a big item (in those days the plants and rocks *were* big—they cost as much as groceries for two months) until you've discussed it together (and agreed on the purchase). Unless you have the cash—money not needed for anything else.

Chapter 3

By the time we celebrated our third anniversary, we felt like we'd arrived. We splurged with dinner on the Top of the Ridpath. Danced to their three piece orchestra. Gazed through the massive windows at the twinkling lights of the city. Romance encircled us like a giant wedding ring.

That Labor Day we put Michele in her crib after lunch and spent a couple of pleasure-filled hours making love—*making* our Stephanie.

My due date was June 5. Dr. Rotchford began titering my blood once a week the first of April. "Don't worry," he said. "I just like to be careful."

But on my birthday, the doctor said, "We've waited long enough. I'm going to induce you day after tomorrow."

My mother was scathing. "If you're going to have that baby early, the least you could do is have it on May 21 (my birthday)!"

I didn't bother the doctor—actually I was kind of happy to keep my birthday *mine*.

Two hours after he gave me the shot, on the morning of May 23, 1960, Stephanie Ann howled her way into our lives. That was the last howl we heard from her until she entered the Terrible Twos. She was so good, one of our friends accused us of *pretending* we had a new baby.

The second Fourth of July, Steve planted the back yard in border-to-border grass. And marked the property lines with a basket-weave wood fence we painted russet.

The bill for the five bushes in front having been long since paid, I actually lobbied for rose plants in the brick planter in front of the living room window and a climbing rose at the base of the chimney on the side. What a joy I felt as I plucked a Cardinal-red bloom, sniffed the intoxicating scent, and placed it in the middle of my dining room table!

That year, as usual, Steve's sister Dodo was visiting us. Not-quite-sixteen, she was in love with Ricky Nelson.

So, when we read in the *Spokesman Review* that the popstar was going to be singing at the Spokane Coliseum, we got three tickets.

Concerts in those days were much more restrained than they are now. There was cheering and we heard lots of *Ricky I love yous*, but the fan noise level didn't punish our eardrums.

Dodo was in heaven—toe-tapping the entire time. When Ricky sang *Travelin' Man*, I swear I thought she'd float right out of her seat.

Later Steve said, "I've never seen Dodo so happy. Why she had a mile-long-smile on her face from the moment we got in the car! All night!"

Years after, when Dodo and I were reminiscing, she told me, "When I got back to Butte that August I was the hit of the neighborhood. 'The funnest thing for us here this summer was the Fourth of July parade,' both Marie and MaryJo complained. 'Ricky Nelson? In person? Boy were you ever lucky!'"

(I wouldn't be surprised if she still has the program. I *know* the memory is tucked in her heart.)

Our new neighborhood—about a mile north of Francis, between Wall and Division—was perfect. In those days, the street dead-ended five houses east of ours at a horse farm. The husbands hand-carted their grass clippings and dropped them just over the fence. The property owner appreciated the fresh fodder. Our kids loved walking up to say "Hi" to the horses.

As our girls grew up, we realized how truly lucky we were. Our kids could walk—ride their trikes and bikes—and play ball in our extra-wide street. Everyone knew everyone. It was truly safe.

When Stephanie was three, I bought her some new red Keds. She wore them all afternoon while riding her trike up and down the little incline from the horse farm to our house singing, "Did you ever go fishing on a bright summer day? With your hands in your pockets and your mouth full of hay?"

Because she used her toes for brakes, by the time she came in for dinner, it looked as if someone had spent hours pulling her new shoes back and forth on a hand-shredder.

Wouldn't you know? That night Steve's mother called saying, "Come home, Pa's had a heart attack." Steve and I put the kids in the back seat in their jammies, grabbed a few clothes, and took off.

It was a false alarm.

The next day, when Steve's father, Pa, took one look at Stephanie's raggedy tennies, he almost blew a gasket. "What's the matter with you, you good-for-nothing?" he yelled at my husband/his son. (I've removed the expletives.) "Can't you even support your family?"

Chapter 3

I was furious! *How dare he talk to his only son like that!* I seethed. *Had he forgotten Steve had to put cardboard in the soles of his shoes when he was little?*

Yet I kept quiet. I'd learned a lesson—you don't cross Pa. Even if you're right.

My dear husband *tried* to explain. His father wouldn't listen. Things were tense.

(And our Butte relatives wondered why we didn't visit more often.)

We bought Stephanie a new pair of shoes as soon as we got back to Spokane—money was *not* a problem. For if Pa had taken the time to listen, he'd have found that Steve was doing well. Very well indeed.

Just before Stephanie was born, he'd taken a job working for a national pharmaceutical company—and doubled our income. It wasn't that we were *rich*. But we'd been really poor the three years he'd been teaching.

With his new job, Steve worked out of town two weeks of every month.

The first week, scared to be in the house all by myself (the only adult) every night, I kept Steve's nine iron under the bed for defense.

By the second week (no one had broken in and tried to have their way with me), I put the club back in Steve's golf bag. (In the light of day, I realized an intruder would grab my so-called weapon and use it on *me*.)

I've got to be brave, I told myself. *Brave and smart.*

My decision? I decided to do something fun that I wouldn't do if Steve were home at night.

It didn't take me long to find the perfect thing—sewing.

I'd put the girls to bed, hurry down to my trusty Pfaff in the family room and sew up a storm. I loved making pretty clothes for me and my kids. (Years later, when making photo albums for Michele and Stephanie, I marveled at the dozens of dresses, coats, and play clothes I'd crafted during those years.)

Often I didn't go to bed until midnight.

Except on the Tuesday night when Dick Van Dyke was on TV.

I planned carefully. Made sure I had a project ready for a half-hour of hand stitching. Watching the clock carefully, I hurried up the basement stairs five minutes before the show began—with fabric, thread, pin cushion, thimble, and scissors—making sure I had plenty of time to settle in.

One night I hadn't watched the time well enough, and only had one minute to make it to the living room TV. Instead of turning on the light at the top of the stairs, I rushed through the kitchen in total blackness. Ran like I was Roger Bannister the day he broke the four minute mile. Forgot about the jog to the left I had to make when I got to the dining room.

Bang!

My nose crashed into what felt like a cement wall. I swear I saw stars.

I dropped everything I was carrying. But being a woman with a purpose, I clicked on the dining room light. Hurried to the TV, and turned it on in time to hear the last bars of the theme song.

It's amazing but true. You can laugh and hold an ice pack on your nose at the same time. I kept the ice on my broken nose for a couple of hours. Took two aspirin. Went to bed.

The next morning I found my scissors on the floor and a gash in the mint-green kitchen paint.

Wow! I thought as I realized how lucky it was that I'd been carrying my scissors pointed away from me. Not at my heart.

When Steve got home I told him how I'd almost killed myself over Dick Van Dyke.

We laughed then. Continued laughing over the years.

Finally, we were able to go out dancing at the Elks. We joined Couples 40, a group that sponsored quarterly dances with a local band. I'd been asked to be a member of Tri Gamma Junior Women's Club, a philanthropic organization that sponsored a ball yearly at the Davenport Hotel and had other socials. Two of our neighboring families were teaching us how to play bridge—alternating weeks. Steve and I were having fun.

Our neighborhood was a great place to have a young family. When it snowed, the city blocked off Washington Street, just a couple of houses west of us, for a sledding hill.

At first we only had one sled. We took turns—Steve with Michele—me with Stephanie. Afterwards we all looked forward to having hot chocolate in our cozy kitchen.

Then, the second year, when both our girls were big enough to sleigh alone, someone left a long Flexible Flyer in our front yard and never came back. After a week, we *borrowed* it. A couple of years later, with no one claiming ownership, we took permanent possession.

Chapter 3

Years later when our daughters dropped sleds for grown-up skies, I sanded The Flyer, stained the wood, and painted the runners bright red. Then I tole-painted a little girl in a red outfit skating on the top.

We started using the new sled for a Christmas decoration in the early seventies. Today, it graces our front entrance, right next to our five-foot St. Francis who, during the holidays, wears a bright red hat topped by a big bell.

The next summer we had a concrete contractor double the size of our patio, and Steve built a cover over the whole thing. We bought two trees. Steve planted them in the middle of the backyard—dreaming of the shade they'd provide in a few years.

Mid-summer, Steve and I decided something was missing. Our new neighbors on the east had filled the dirt borders on three sides of their backyard with plants and perennials. By July they had a plethora of color. We wanted some blooming flowers too.

But how? Our lawn grew right to the wood fence on three sides.

"We need to dig out the grass," I suggested. "Probably three feet. All around."

"Do you realize how much work that'd be?" Steve retaliated. "That stuff is thick."

Our neighbor Dick heard of our dilemma. He said, "If you can wait until next summer, I've got an idea for you. My neighbor in Seattle had the same problem. This is what he did—just mark the area you want to turn into a flower bed, take a sharp shovel, and cut all the grass in two-foot squares. Then turn and plop it—root side up. By next spring, the grass will have died and turned into compost—instant fertilizer."

That fall, we designed our flower garden. Steve dug generous scallops on both sides and the back. Followed directions. Turned. Plopped.

By spring, when it was time to work in the yard, Steve was working out of town. Week after week.

So—determined to have my flower garden—I approached our backyard holding a trowel in my right hand and enthusiasm for the project in my heart.

Long story short—my right hand begin aching by noon, and my heart had relocated itself somewhere south—probably to my toes.

While I know the basis of the theory to be correct—matter does decay—I think it would have taken a good twenty years to reach the goal of rich loam from upside-down-grass.

Undeterred, I dug. Got a one-foot square free. Attacked it with the trowel—no progress. Moved to a pointed shovel—about the same. In disgust, I shook off what soil I could—not more than a thimble full.

Impossible! I thought. *There's got to be a way.* I could *see* those flowers in my mind's eye.

Determined, for the next two weeks, five days a week, I spent at least four hours each day working on our flower garden. I dug—shook as much loose dirt from of each individual piece of sod as possible—threw the rest in our wheelbarrow—pushed it a half block to the open area at the end of our street available to such excess—and dumped.

I must say, I had a few choice words for our neighbor—but I kept quiet. I don't know which was harder—keeping my frustration to myself—or the actual physical work.

Whatever—come mid-May we bought several flats of petunias—half purple—half white. The finished product was worth it!

In July I hosted a luncheon for twenty-four members of my women's club in our new backyard garden. I provided ice cream cake for dessert and basked in the compliments I received.

On that long-ago day, on Cascade Way, I discovered two of my favorite things—entertaining and flowers.

As our seventh anniversary arrived, Steve made reservations for Friday and Saturday in the brand new Desert Inn in downtown Spokane. He'd planned a celebration for just the two of us—a Friday night at the Elk's Country Club dining room at Liberty Lake, a day of shopping, and dinner at the Ridpath Roof on Saturday. Dancing both evenings.

"It'll be a second honeymoon," he promised.

All I had to do was get a babysitter. My parents lived one house away. They would have been happy to have our daughters move in with them permanently.

But, when I explained what Steve and I wanted to do for our big day and asked for forty-eight hours room and board for my girls, my mother looked as if I'd told her I was going to hire myself out as a call-girl for the weekend.

"Well I never!" she huffed. "Never in a million years would I have thought *my* daughter would do anything like *that*!"

Chapter 3

I felt like saying, "I've been married for seven years for heaven's sake! I have two children. What do you think? That I got pregnant sitting on a toilet seat? Twice?"

But I kept my cool.

My mother finally condescended to be my babysitter for a long weekend date with my husband.

When I dropped the kids off on Friday afternoon, I was greeted with an ice-cube-stare.

I forgot my mother the minute we backed out of our driveway.

Steve and I had a delightful, romantic anniversary weekend. Dined and danced, lunched and shopped, dined and danced again.

On Sunday morning, we went to Mass at St. Al's—my very favorite church in the whole world. After brunch, we ended up the three-day event by playing nine holes of golf at Wandermere on Sunday afternoon.

Introduced to my first Frango mint that long ago time—the Desert Inn had placed a complimentary box on our pillow—I became addicted. To this day, when I pop a Frango in my mouth, I remember the joy of *that* weekend. And my forty-eight hours living on the wild side with my dear husband, my lover Steve.

In the seven years we lived on Cascade Way, we made life-time friends. (Right now I'm on Facebook with five of my lady-friend's children.) We had kid's birthday parties—too many to count, Easter egg hunts, backyard barbecues.

Not one of the ladies on the street worked. (I'd quit just before Stephanie was born.) We had lots of evening get-togethers.

But I came to especially look forward to having coffee with special neighbors Monday through Friday, from 11:00 to noon. They became like the sisters I'd never had.

One family, the Watanabes, liked the location so well they rented not one but two different houses before they built a split-level down Washington Hill and over a block.

I spent many an hour drinking coffee at my friend Laura's house while my Stephanie and her Barbie played in the family room.

The girls must have worn out one record—*Puff the Magic Dragon*.

Just recently, during a TV tribute to Peter, Paul and Mary, I suddenly heard the duo singing the familiar words.

I hummed the tune... Remembered... Teared up...

Nostalgia captured my heart.

For a minute I was in Honalee. It was magic.

My friend Laura still lives in the same house—down Washington Street—on Sierra Way. She loves entertaining her grandkids in the backyard swimming pool. A couple of Octobers ago, I spent an afternoon visiting with Laura and another friend, Susie, who had moved to another neighborhood. What a fun time we had!

But all good things end. Or change.

Steve took what was supposed to be a dream job—President of McClintock Drilling. They sent him to the main office in New York City. On a three-week tour through Nevada and Arizona. Back to New York. They went broke.

One day, the week Steve heard the news about McClintock folding, I'd just come back from appointments with two doctors. "You've got pink eye," the Ear, Eyes, and Throat MD told me. My OB/GYN said, "You've got a vaginal infection."

My mother chose that time to drop by. She found me in the back yard. Worrying.

"Blah, blah, blah," my mother complained.

I tried to block her out.

She continued.

At the end of my rope, devastated because of Steve's recent unemployment, hurting at two ends of my body, I finally interrupted and said, "Mother, I have troubles too."

"You?" she whined before I could even tell her my medical problems. "Why, you have the best furniture of anyone on the block!" With that, she flounced off.

So, when Steve got a new job (a couple of days later) that began as an insurance salesman for Allstate at the Northtown Mall in north Spokane and quickly became a district manager trainee, eligible for reassignment to another city when the training ended, I rejoiced. I was ready to move. (I knew my parents were not financially able to follow us—the company would pay all our moving expenses—not those of any one else.)

Our home sold, and we bought a new place in Tacoma.

Chapter 3

When push came to shove, I knew I'd miss my friends like crazy. But . . .

Just before we were scheduled to leave, the neighborhood ladies had a going-away party for me. That night, the truth came out.

"You know, Darlene," one said, "when you first moved in—with your toddler and Dodo—we all thought Dodo was Steve's daughter by a first marriage. (Steve had always looked very mature—one of the reasons I was attracted to him.) All of us were shocked when we found she was his sister."

Everyone had a big laugh over that.

As the movers packed the final boxes, the boss said, "I really feel sorry for you. Moving from a beautiful house like this—from such a great neighborhood."

I must admit, I shed a few tears as we left.

It had been a truly wonderful seven years.

Chapter 4

"You're moving where?" people asked.

"It's kind of hard to say," I'd answered. "Steve's office is in Tacoma. And, technically, we'll live in Tacoma. But . . .

"The (unincorporated) area is called Lakewood. We briefly stayed in the Lakewood Motor Inn the Friday night the girls and I arrived on the plane. We ate at The Lakewood Terrace. But our house is in a new housing project called Oakbrook. So—take your pick."

The mover's first word as he walked in our new home was, "Wow!" Followed quickly with, "Can't believe it. This is even nicer than the one you left in Spokane."

I must admit, in January 1966—the evening we first drove down Emerald Drive and I saw the glitzy, billboard-sized sign advertising *Oakbrook*—I thought, *Wait a minute. We can't afford this!*

Sensing my distress, Steve said, "Bob just invited us for dinner. He's a district manager. Just like me."

"He must be independently wealthy," I fussed.

After we feasted on lobster cooked by Bob's wife Drew, we discovered he'd made an appointment the next morning for an Oakbrook real estate salesman to show us houses.

I worried *What have we gotten ourselves into?*

As happened before when I worried, Steve kissed me quiet.

Next morning, the first house we looked at was just up the street from Bob's, a not-quite-finished split-level with a shake roof, brown cedar siding, trimmed in used brick. Beautiful!

Chapter 4

I tried not to drool as the salesman took us down a long, tiled entrance hall into a huge living room with a floor-to-ceiling brick fireplace. He continued to a separate dining room and a generous kitchen with a large eating area. Two sliding glass doors opened onto a back yard that looked like a forest. About ten feet from the house was a rock wall that went from one side of the lot to the other—excluding the stairs.

The upper level featured three bedrooms and two baths. Down six steps was a big family room—with a corner fireplace, bathroom, laundry room, and an unfinished space—perfect for a fourth bedroom/den/sewing room—that only requiring paneling and flooring.

"And a real plus," the salesman said, "is that the buyer can choose the paint colors for all the walls, plus the flooring in the kitchen, bathrooms, and lower level. The bedrooms, living room, and dining room will be solid oak."

I tried to stay cool—I loved to decorate. "How much?"

"Just $26,000." (This was in 1966.)

"Too much money," we said.

All that Saturday we looked at other homes in Oakbrook. We'd planned on driving up to Seattle for a special dinner after our house-shopping. By dusk, we were so tired we walked across the street to the nearest restaurant from our motel—The Lakewood Terrace. (It turned out to be a gift in disguise. The Terrace, as it's called locally, turned out to be the best restaurant in the Tacoma/ Lakewood/University Place area.)

After church the next morning, we set out on our own. We found a couple of possible neighborhoods, called the phone numbers on the signs—they started at $10,000 more than the Oakbrook house we loved.

We tried a real estate agent in University Place. Prices were the same or more than the one on Emerald Drive we thought we couldn't afford.

We agonized.

Steve quoted the regional manager's house-buying advice: "Buy like you'll live there forever. You're on your way up, Steve. Don't chintz."

When we walked into the Oakbrook Real Estate office that Sunday afternoon at a quarter to five, our real estate guy was waiting for us.

If I could have moved my friend Laura next door, I would have called it heaven.

The afternoon we moved in, we had a visitor—Gus Krepela—complete with his wheelbarrow holding three azaleas he'd grown from seed.

"Just a little welcoming present," Gus said. He proceeded to plant his prize-winning plants where they'd be the focal point of view from our kitchen.

"Come down and meet my wife Lynn when you get settled," he said when he finished.

Gus, a big burly man who looked like a gardener with his rough clothes and dirt-under-the-nails hands was one of Steve's agents. They lived just down the street on the end of Oakbrook Lane.

It was the beginning of a beautiful friendship.

The first Monday, the doorbell rang. I opened the front door to find a smile and a plate of fresh-from-the-oven chocolate chip cookies. "I'm Janet Andrews," said the lady I surmised was about my age. "I live just down the street. The yellow house with the red-brick trim. Some of the neighbor ladies are having a meeting this Thursday evening to start up a Junior Women's Club," my new neighbor said. "Would you like to join me?"

(That didn't take much thinking. I'd just left Spokane in the middle of my second term as president of Tri Gama Junior Women's Club.)

On Thursday, I got acquainted with Janet, Sandy Luttinen and Karen Fowler (who, with their husbands, made the core of the six-couple bridge group we'd start that fall), and a dozen other delightful women my age.

While Steve and I may have acclimated socially, and while we loved the neighborhood, all was not perfect in Paradise.

The day we moved in, I was in the main bathroom upstairs cleaning the tub (it was filled with debris and sawdust) when I heard Steve shouting. I could hear panic in his voice.

My God, I thought. *Something terrible must have happened.* I rushed out the bathroom. Tore down two flights of stairs.

As I made the turn, I heard two things: Steve shouting, "*Turn it off!*" And the sound of gushing water. We had a flood rushing from the ceiling of our downstairs bath.

"Are you running water in the upstairs bathtub?" Steve asked when I peeked in.

"Of course. We can't use it the way it is. What's that got to . . .

Chapter 4

"Well get yourself back upstairs and turn it off! The plumber must have forgotten to hook up the drain!"

No one got baths that evening. Here we were in a brand new, three-bathroom house with no tub and only one shower that worked (the one in the flooded bathroom wasn't finished).

Oakbrook Realty got a plumber out the next day. We never got a bill—for which I was glad—plumbers are always expensive, and they probably charged triple on Sunday.

FHA came to inspect a couple of weeks later and refused to close our loan.

"Your house isn't finished," they told us. "There's no bullnose on the top of the stairs, no guardrail on the back stairway, the shower in the downstairs bath isn't useable, and the ceiling has to be replaced."

We'd never even met the man who built our house, so we contacted our real estate agent who said, "Well, we have a little problem. The builder had some money difficulties, and he's nowhere to be found."

Your problem, not ours, I thought. Steve agreed. We waited. And waited. Nothing.

Two months later, the manager of Oakbrook Realty arrived at our front door with a smile and a rental agreement—retroactive to our move-in date.

"You've been living here for two and a half months," he said. "Free."

"I really can't help that," Steve answered. "We were ready to sign the final papers on day one. The bank won't sign off until FHA provides them a completion document. We gave our agent the list of what needs to be fixed months ago. Our lender won't budge until everything's done.

"I'm not going to sign a rental agreement, but I'll be more than happy to sign the final loan papers when the bank gives us the okay."

A week later the house was completely finished. Soon after, FHA inspected and approved.

We lucked out. With the money we saved on not paying a house payment for three months, we bought carpet for our living room, dining room, and master bedroom.

༄

I was twenty-nine. Only days before I turned thirty.

I felt as if I were seventy-nine, almost eighty. Far past the age when I could do something worthwhile.

Two years before I'd been denied the opportunity to go to my tenth high school reunion—something I'd really anticipated. Steve had just lost his position at the company that went bankrupt, gotten a new job, and was in a month-long training program in California.

Thinking I couldn't go without my husband, I pouted. During that period, I began thinking of what my high school biology/chemistry teacher, Mr. Nelson, had said.

"If you haven't made it by the time you're thirty, you'd better resign yourself to being a failure."

He'd said this after spending fifty-five minutes chastising my friend Darlene Jenson for misspelling the word aluminum in a test. He finished his barrage of derision and turned to the rest of us.

"I see a lot of potential failures in this class," he prophesied.

Walking around the room, he looked each of us in the eye. I felt he spent an extra minute when he stood in front of me—like he'd prejudged my future, and I'd failed his test.

I spent my lunch hour crying.

Here I was—nearly thirty. I had to admit to myself—in Mr. Nelson's eyes—I was a failure. I'd quit college to marry Steve. I wasn't an engineer, a doctor, or a dentist—the only professions Mr. Nelson touted as being important. Why, I wasn't even a teacher or a nurse (second best, but the only jobs my nemesis-teacher said girls could aspire to).

True, I'd just moved into a beautiful home and was in the process of decorating it. I sewed almost everything the girls and I wore. I'd upholstered sofas and chairs, made draw-drapes, wall-papered three bathrooms and the entry hall since February. And started making a quilt for our queen-size bed. I had two smart daughters who were doing me proud in school.

As president of Tri Gamma, I'd walked up to the podium during the state convention of the Washington State Junior Women's Clubs at the Olympic Hotel in Seattle. I'd accepted the 1964 award for community service—a humongous silver bowl simply called the *Gyllenburg*. (The award was a tribute to Charlotte Gyllenburg who, in 1935, had become the first president of the Junior Federation of the General Federation of Women's Clubs.)

I remember tracing the inscription on that bowl—GYLLENBURG—with my index finger and thinking of the motto our group said at the beginning of each meeting.

I pledge my loyalty to the Junior Club women,

Chapter 4

By doing better than ever before
What work I have to do,
By being prompt, honest, courteous,
By living each day, trying to accomplish something,
Not merely to exist.

It had been a proud moment. I adopted the "living each day, trying to accomplish something, not merely to exist" as my mantra.

But I could just hear Mr. Nelson's retort, "That's different." He made "different" sound like a dirty word.

Yes, I felt sorry for myself. I was lonely. I missed my five-day-a-week, hour-every-day coffee klatch with my friend Laura—solving the problems of the world. And our own.

My husband loved his new job. My daughters had assimilated beautifully. But me? Sometimes I felt like I was Alice tumbling down the rabbit hole.

I remembered April of 1964—when I was working full-time on finishing up our Junior Women's Club project, writing the state reports, and working on the next dance sponsored by Couples Fifty.

One night I didn't get home from my last meeting until almost 5 p.m. (I wasn't worried about my daughters—Steve's sister was visiting us).

When Steve arrived at 5:15 looking for dinner, I could have climbed into a hole had one been available.

I couldn't believe my negligence—*I'd completely forgotten to cook dinner!*

The girls and Dodo were okay with peanut butter sandwiches, canned peaches, and oatmeal cookies and ice cream for dessert.

Steve was not.

Dinner conversation was nil.

After I put the girls to bed, I attempted to placate Steve.

"There's a great movie on TV tonight," I said. "A comedy called *Rally Round the Flag, Boys!* With Paul Newman and Joanne Woodward. Why don't I pop some popcorn, and we can watch the movie together? Have a few laughs."

Steve went downstairs to the family room with me. He turned on the TV. We ate some popcorn.

Fifteen minutes into the movie, Steve threw his hands up.

"And they call this comedy?" he yelled. "It's my life! And I can tell you it's *not* funny."

He stormed upstairs.

Two years later Steve had forgiven me. But—remembering Mr. Nelson's words—I groveled in self-pity.

Steve hadn't made any special plans for my "big" day. No, "Let's celebrate your birthday by going to Seattle for a big night out." Nothing!

So I made plans of my own. I invited my new friend Janet and her husband over for an evening of bridge. I'd made my very-favorite-in-the-whole-world dessert—ice cream cake—for the occasion.

I had my new hairdresser at Rhodes *do* my hair. Always something I enjoyed.

Those days, Steve often spent part of his Saturdays at the Sears store, checking out the fifteen Allstate agents he managed. My birthday that Saturday was no different.

I met Steve at the door with a kiss when he got home—like I always did.

He handed me a big sack emblazoned with the logo—SEARS.

"Happy birthday," he said.

I blanched. Reached in the paper bag and pulled out what, apparently, was my thirtieth birthday present—a garish print mumu. Not even wrapped.

I have no memory of what I said. Probably not nice.

I cried.

Dinner was a disaster. I have no idea what I cooked. I do remember the absolute silence. Even Michele and Stephanie were afraid to say a word. They *knew*. Mom was furious at Dad—on her birthday.

By 8:00, I'd put on a new dress I'd just made. Set up the card table in the middle of the living room. Double checked—saw the cards and score pad ready to use, snacks, napkins in place. It looked like I didn't have a worry in the world.

When Janet and Gordy arrived, I was all smiles. We had a fun evening.

The next day, after almost ten years of marriage, Steve began to tell me some of his family secrets. Things he'd hidden for fear I'd think badly of him.

Birthdays were often not happy events at his childhood home. One especially haunted him. Shouting. Fist banging on the table. Steve being the recipient of his father's derision.

Chapter 4

His mother always made him a special dessert—like his favorite, banana cream pie. But, presents—never. Even at Christmas he was lucky to get a crumpled five-dollar bill—definitely not wrapped and bowed. He'd never even had a birthday party!

I was shocked.

We talked. Learned much more about each other than we'd ever known before.

The next Tuesday Steve arrived home from work with a beautifully wrapped box. "Happy birthday," he said. My dear husband had called a friend in Spokane who owned a clothing store at the Northtown Mall who'd overnighted a special-delivery package to his office.

I opened the box to find a beautiful pair of slacks and matching top—in one of my favorite colors—pale pink. Perfect.

Both Steve and I learned something the year I turned thirty.

He never again gave me a gift in a paper bag. (In fact, his increasingly lovely presents were always professionally wrapped.)

I learned to listen to my husband—and not just while he was talking. I found silence could sometimes be more revealing than chatter.

Together, we grew.

⸺

The card-playing lessons we'd recently enjoyed in Spokane gave us an entrée to local social life. Our right-in-the back neighbors, Liz and Dick, invited Steve and me for a new-to-us evening out—dinner and bridge. Dinner was delicious. Company—two other new-in-town couples—lively. Our card-playing seemed to be working (I must admit, I'd been a little nervous).

It wasn't until later that I got *the rest of the story*.

"You'll never believe this," Steve began when we got home. "In the last game, I counted my cards and almost died. I had opening count—18 points!"

"Wow," I said. "What did you make on the hand?"

"Let me tell you—the final score is *not* the point," he said.

"My opponent, Paula, bid three no trump to open. (According to Goren's bridge rules, you need 25 to 27 points to bid that.) My partner passed. Paula's husband Rex, her partner for this set, went to four. (Rules said you need 10 to 14 points.) I figured they were loaded for bear and passed.

"Without batting an eyelash, Paula said, 'Seven no trump.'"

"'Come on, Paula!' her husband complained.

"Paula's eyes got like two slits. She growled, '*Shut-up and play your cards!*'

"Rex put down a heart—my good suit—and the rest is history. We took every trick. Set them. Made 1,500 points."

Ever since that night, if either of us says or does something *very* inappropriate, the other deadpans and says, "Shut up and play your cards!" Nothing else is necessary—those six words are the perfect squelch.

Our girls loved Oakbrook too. Although we moved in February, they quickly fit in.

One thing Oakbrook had going for it was the pool. Less than a half block from our house was a well-managed, Olympic-size, community pool. Membership was minimal—we paid gladly. (Steve ended up being on the board soon after.)

We Moms never had to worry. The manager was loved by the kids and admired by the parents. He hired local teens as lifeguards (Michele made that her first job years later). They had a swim team that practiced every day and competed in Amateur Athletic Union (AAU) swim meets all summer. (Our girls joined the second year—the first year they just took lessons and had fun.)

Every summer the grown-ups had a pool party. I still have the picture of the first one—a luau. I made Steve a lava-lava sarong—he went bare chested. I wore the cover-up from Sears that Steve gave me for my birthday. Janet's husband Gordie got feisty and jumped in the pool—forgetting to take off his new wristwatch. (Bet he never did *that* again!)

Besides the Junior Women's Club (of which Karen, Janet, and I would all eventually become president), I joined the Lakewood Transplants (garden club), and the Newcomer's Club. Newcomers had events every Wednesday—monthly lunch meeting, bridge and crafts on the other weeks. Besides there were additional neighborhood bridge groups (loved mine) and lots of evening things with husbands.

Steve and I joined the brand new Oakbrook Golf & Country Club. Steve golfed on Saturdays—I joined the Nine Hole group on Thursdays. Often Steve and I played nine holes after dinner. We went to dances and balls.

I was a social butterfly—loved it. Yet, I could always be at home when the girls got out of school.

Chapter 4

As the holiday season approached, I realized we had a new problem—a stack of invitations.

"What should we do?" I asked Steve. "We've been invited to six Christmas cocktail parties already."

"I wouldn't call that a problem," Steve said. "It sounds like fun."

"Well, we can't just *go*. We have to reciprocate. And I don't know how to make a single fancy hors d'oeuvre."

"Serve cheese and crackers."

"Yeah, right. The only kind of cheese my mother ever bought was Velveeta. And neither one of us can stand *that*. Besides, the parties we've already gone to have tables of delicacies that look like something from the December *Better Homes and Gardens*. Not just cheese and crackers."

Steve thought a while and finally said, "Why don't we do something different? Remember when we had breakfast after one of those Couples Forty dances? That went off great. You made homemade cinnamon rolls, and I scrambled eggs. We served ham."

"Hmm," I said. "We could add your mother's povetica (Croatian nut bread). Maybe I could put out a couple of my fancy Christmas cookies. Serve champagne punch besides coffee and tea. "

"Sounds great," Steve said. "Thank goodness we have a big freezer."

I began stockpiling.

When we moved, we'd trashed the aluminum tree our family had used for seven years. Steve and I thought the revolving colored light that sat underneath was festive—the girls hated it. They won.

I began checking our Christmas ornaments and realized the dozen original glass balls we'd bought ten years before were all we had. I envisioned a seven-foot tree.

"We need more," I wailed. "Lots more!"

Steve came to the rescue. He said, "I heard of the perfect place to buy Christmas decorations. It's in downtown Tacoma—a place called Ghilarducci's."

One noon, Steve took me to lunch, and then we went to the flower shop with the Italian name. We walked up a curved white staircase and found a second-floor fairyland.

I bought detail-rich ornaments—children dressed in red riding white swans, sweet little mice tucked in their beds, angels in colorful dresses, even elephants. Red and white check fabric was used to trim them all—even the beautiful angel that made the perfect tree topper. *After all these years, my red-check Ghilarducci ornaments are still the first ones I hang every Christmas.*

I *had* made one new decoration the last year we were in Spokane—a Christmas family—Styrofoam balls for heads connected to cone-shaped bodies. A father, mother, and two children, they were dressed in red flannel stocking caps and nightgowns with sleeves stuffed with paper to make arms. They graced our fireplace mantle.

And, of course, we'd display our special five choir boys. But . . .

I started looking at magazines for ideas. *Better Homes and Gardens* had two dandies—a Christmas castle and some angel cutouts to hang outside.

Steve's creative side surfaced. He turned the garage into Santa's workplace at the North Pole.

First he cut two angels out of plywood to hang on our living room shutters—a head, body, and wings. I covered the head with golden curls and smiling faces (thanks to the magic of felt) and the bodies with little red and green dresses.

The castle started off as a piece of plywood. Steve cut a floor and three flat sides. On the fourth—the front—he crafted a curved arch with a drawbridge made from the cut out.

Steve painstakingly cut crenellations—derived from the French word *creneler* which means to furnish the battlements with diminutive notches or crannies—at the top of all four sides. In Medieval castles the purpose of these gaps was to give a good vantage point from which soldiers could launch their arrows. In Steve's version, they were for decoration—and a grand decoration they were.

Turrets finished each of the four corners. *How do I make a turret?* Steve agonized. (*Better Homes and Gardens* didn't provide directions.) Remembering the carpet we'd bought that spring, he went to the flooring store and asked, "How much for a couple of the cardboard spools your carpet comes on?"

"Take as many as you want," he was told. "We just throw 'em out."

It was no small job fitting the cylinders so they melded perfectly against the ninety-degree-angles of the four corners. But he measured and

Chapter 4

cut and measured and cut until each fit closely. Then he glued each turret against the wood.

Next he made a mezzanine across the back side of the inside. That done, he gave the whole thing several coats of bright white paint—inside and out.

Then he gave it to me and said, "Do your magic."

I found paper that looked like stained glass, cut it in long, narrow rectangles with curved tops, and created two windows on each turret.

Our daughters were young in those days, and Sears still put out a Christmas toy catalogue where I found the perfect furniture. The piece de résistance was a white baby grand piano—complete with a red-velvet covered bench. It also included a white buffet (with tiny gold knobs on the three bottom drawers and three additional shelves behind a glassed door on the top), four red-velvet covered dining room chairs, a tiny table, a celery-green satin curved sofa, a hassock, and two end tables.

I decided to add a bedroom and made a king-sized bed. It featured a headboard made of stiff pearl edging and a red satin bedspread.

Steve carpeted the castle floor and mezzanine with red felt.

The focal point was the throne—complete with a queen and king (made of round-topped clothespins and imagination).

I made pointed turret roofs with felted poster board and topped them with red felt flags glued to toothpicks. For ten years, this handcrafted castle brought magic to the Matule Christmas.

In 1966 we began our Christmas family tradition—an annual brunch for friends and a house decorated with whimsy. And lots of love!

One evening as we were having a glass of wine before dinner, Steve said, "You know, Darlene, I feel guilty taking money for doing my job—I like it so much."

I quickly assured him that his employer *expected* to pay him. (I kept cool—didn't emphasize that we had a house payment, groceries, and little things like that I had to pay with his salary since we weren't independently wealthy.)

Besides—he worked hard. Eight to five, then back to Lakewood for dinner with the family. After kissing the girls good-night, he was back again on appointments with his salesmen and their clients. I always waited up for him.

Steve's work paid off. In May 1968 he was chosen to go to the Allstate Honor Ring-Conference of Champions at the Hotel del Coronado in San Diego—a real honor.

To get my wardrobe ready I made a trip to the fabric department at Frederick & Nelson in Seattle. That resulted in an aqua lace ball gown, a white linen suit, three Vogue (intricately designed patterns) dresses, and a four-piece sports ensemble.

My folks came from Spokane to baby-sit. We were gone seven days—a combination San Diego and Las Vegas vacation. Wonderful!

In Vegas we never gambled. Just ate delicious meals and saw all the floor shows we could—Tony Bennett, Vic Damon, the Follies Bergere, Phil Harris and Alice Faye, Steve Lawrence and Eydie Gorme, Trini Lopez, Vaughn Monroe, Wayne Newton, Juliet Prowse, Joan Rivers, and Andy Williams.

Yet there was a hole in my persona. At that point in our marriage, I was *not* Steve's everything. He had a separate life—his work. And I respected that. Actually envied it.

Although I had never heard of the word—*synchronicity*—it didn't wait for my awareness to begin working to make my life better.

Carl Jung, who is credited in discovering the phenomenon, had several different definitions over the years. The one I connect with most is: *Synchronicity is the fortuitous intermeshing of events.*

In 1968, three events collided: Oakbrook . . . Steve's work ethic . . . And my search for a meaning for my life . . .

Synchronicity arrived in three special Oakbrook friends.

As I write this, I ask myself, *What makes Lynn and Janet and Grace more special than other friends?*

The answer: They're *gone.*

Remembering them makes me realize how precious life is. Losing them taught me to cherish my friends who are still here. As I mourned these three women at their funerals, I also celebrated my memories of our times together. Each of them shaded my life, teaching me new facets of love.

Chapter 4

Lynn

Lynn was old enough to be my mother. Unlike my birth-mother, she and Gus were openly affectionate. *What a lovely couple!* I thought the first time I saw them together.

When I admired her husband Gus's forsythia plant, she drove me out to Buckley Nursery to buy one of my own. She taught me how to make dill pickles, starting with scouting out the best place to buy the right size cucumbers, driving me to the local St. Vincent DePaul to buy my Kerr canning jars, and right on through the first day of *pickling.*

She hosted many *adult only* dinners, introducing Steve and me to new favorites. For me, it was an easy, yet elegant, hors d'oeuvre—shrimp cocktail. For Steve—beer-basted ham roast. We still use both recipes.

And cookies—Lynn was a master. While she'd never had children, she knew how to make kids happy. She always had a cookie jar filled for our girls.

All these years later, memories of Lynn invade my kitchen every Christmas as I bake my family's favorite cookies—her Prayer Bars and Seven Story Bars. Steve and I love the Scandinavian goody she reintroduced me to—yummy, buttery Spritz.

But one spring afternoon, after we'd been living in Oakbrook seven years, I heard that Gus, only fifty-nine and ready to retire the coming January, had suffered a heart attack.

When Steve got home, he called Lynn and said, "If there's anything I can do, please let me know."

Two hours later she called us. "I'm at the hospital. Waiting for news about Gus. Can you come?"

We left our teenagers and hurried to Lakewood General where we held Lynn's hand. We had a long wait.

Finally the doctor arrived. Lynn stood up. You could see the hope in her eyes.

"He's dead," the MD said in a voice as cold and hard as sleet. "What funeral home do you want?"

At that moment, Steve and I adopted Lynn.

Steve gently asked and got a name of the Puyallup mortuary her family used. We took her back to Oakbrook Lane—where every step was a reminder of her beloved Gus.

Calling all her family and other friends, Steve began making the necessary preparations. Then he went home to be with our daughters.

I stayed overnight, not wanting her to be alone. I slept in the guest room—in my slip.

That night I prayed a new prayer—one I've said twice a day since.

Please, please, please Lord Jesus,
Make it possible for Steve and me to be able to live together
for many, many, many years to come,
Happy with each other, healthy in mind and body.

The next morning neither Steve nor I went to our offices.

We helped Lynn make funeral arrangements—choose the casket, decide on a cemetery lot. We found the perfect place to bury him—right under a blooming, brilliant-red rhododendron. For the first time that day, Lynn smiled.

From then on until the day she died of emphysema almost twenty years later, Lynn always had her *day-after-holiday* dinners with us (her relatives hosted Christmas, etc.) And in between, lots of other *just because* dinners. Like clockwork she'd arrive at our house at four and leave at eight. We loved her—like a mother. Her birthday, January 7, is still celebrated with a special meal at our house

Janet

A stay-at-home mom, Janet had three kids, and a baby.

We became bosom buddies. So close, she loaned me her sterling silver flatware when Steve and I had sit-down dinners for his crew of agents and their wives (at the time I didn't realize what an honor that was). We had lots of cups of tea over the years (mostly at her house because she had the youngest child). And lots of *girl talk*.

Together we organized the Oakbrook Garden Club. I remember one day especially—the meeting at Janet's—me in charge of dessert. Right after I'd put my cake into the oven, I went out to get the mail. Got locked out. With no keys, I was homeless and carless.

I ran to her house with my horror story. Without a "How could you be so dumb?" Janet drove me downtown to Steve's office where I got a house key. Then she zoomed us back in time to get my cake out of the oven just as the timer rang.

Chapter 4

When I got to her house just before noon, the dining room was set with china and sterling. Multiple fresh-flower arrangements brought the scent of spring inside. No one had a clue about our scurrying earlier. Thanks to Janet.

The first fall we started a once-a-month couple's bridge group. We played *conversation* bridge and had so much fun that the six couples also spent New Year's Eve together for years—alternating houses. And, because four couples shared August wedding anniversaries, we had a yearly celebration dinner at a special restaurant.

When I began tole-painting, Janet joined me for weekly art lessons. (We still decorate our Christmas tree with tole-painted wooden ornaments—Mr. and Mrs. Santa Claus, Raggedy Ann and Andy, and three different views of angels (one playing a harp, another flying, and the third singing). I made three of each. When Steve and I made our last move, I found a Christmas dwarf that Janet had painted tucked away in my Christmas stuff. Janet's son Greg was thrilled when I gave it to him. His house had recently burned to the ground, and they lacked any family mementoes. *Synchronicity in action.*

Janet and I picked strawberries every June—accompanied by our kids. Cost? Twenty-five cents a pound. What times we had! Lots of strawberry smeared faces.

For twenty years, Janet and I were best of friends—before ovarian cancer claimed her life just before she turned fifty. During all those years—through business ups and downs—through kid problems (and she had more than her share)—up to the very night before she died when we enjoyed a couple of hours visiting and drinking tea—I never heard Janet complain.

When my first grandson was born, she arrived at my door with a small bouquet of flowers in a cup decorated with the words, *World's Greatest Grandma*. I use it often. And, always when I do, I feel Janet's presence.

Recently I attended the wedding of Janet's granddaughter where I enjoyed dinner sitting between two of her children. What a privilege!

Last Christmas, when Steve and I were at Stephanie's for the holiday, Greg drove over from Gig Harbor with one of his daughters, especially to visit with Steve and me. I was thrilled to find the once near juvenile delinquent—who had shredded my yellow-rose hedge and blamed it on another kid—had become a knowledgeable, caring, upstanding dad.

Afterwards, I sent a little prayer up to Janet. "Greg's looking good. You can be proud." I felt the warmth of her smile.

Grace

Grace Olsen moved across from our home on Emerald Drive probably five years after we arrived from Spokane. The first thing she did was paint her front door bright Chinese red. Grace had style.

Probably five or six years younger than I was at the time, Grace was super friendly. As a brand new neighbor, Grace and her husband Ray often invited us over for *just a snack*. We enjoyed their company.

But it seemed that every time she called to suggest a night out for the four of us, we were always busy. It happened so often I finally told Steve, "I'm afraid our new neighbor thinks I'm just making excuses. Every time she calls I turn her down."

Then one night Steve answered the phone. I heard him say, "We'd love to join you." I could hardly wait to hear what we were going to do.

Not even cracking a smile, he said. "We're going to Puyallup with Grace and Ray for Chinese food."

"You hate Chinese," I reminded him.

"Well, I like the Olsens. I'll just suffer. I'm afraid if we turned them down one more time they'd quit asking."

I almost lost it later when he admitted, "That was great. Let's go again soon."

Chalk up one for Grace, I thought.

We started doing a lot with our new neighbors.

Years later, Grace hosted a dinner party to celebrate their move into a new house a few blocks away that her contractor husband had just built. To my dismay, she served acorn squash. I'd hated squash since I was in third grade and forced to eat it at a friend's house when I was staying over. (Her dad had a razor strop in the bathroom that I'd been told came out when dinners weren't finished.) Steve had never even tasted it.

We chose to be polite—and were astounded. *We liked squash!*

Thank you, Grace, for introducing Chinese food and squash to the Matule diet!

Stephanie was a staple of the Olsen household—she mowed their lawn and babysat their three daughters, Tonya, Karlena, and Vanessa. She

Chapter 4

enjoyed the money, but I think she'd have taken care of the kids for nothing—she loved those girls.

Then Grace got breast cancer. She fought valiantly. Although she lost all her hair from treatments, all we ever saw were the blond curls of her latest wig (she had several). She never complained. One evening when we visited her at the hospital, instead of fussing about her limited diet, I remember her extoling a glass of milk. Plain milk—not chocolate—not a milkshake. She died at age thirty-five.

Lately, I see Grace's oldest daughter, Tonya, often at Stephanie's house. (Steph took the time to search her out on Facebook and re-connect.)

Steve and I never have Chinese food or squash without thinking of Grace. When I go past the duplex Grace's husband built for my folks when they could no longer live on their own in Spokane, I remember Grace's beautiful smile.

And every year when Tonya mentions her mother's birthday on Facebook, I always *Like* and add, "Happy Birthday, Grace. I miss you."

But after four years of near bliss, I must admit, I got bored.

While keeping a *Mrs. Clean* house, (I had it down to a system) I was done with my cleaning most every morning at 10 a.m. There wasn't something going on every day. The girls were at school. Nights, Steve was often out with his agents—working.

"I'm bored," I told Steve. "I'm going to get a job."

He had a fit. "I make enough money. You don't *have* to work. Besides, my father would disown me—he thinks men who make their wives work are (in Steve's father's words) worthless *sons-of-bitches*."

We argued. He talked to one of the adjustors at work who told him that his wife had been the same. She'd gotten a job, and they were both happy. Finally, Steve said, "Well, you just do it. Get a job." (Like he was sure no one would hire me.)

I fooled him—got a job in the Personnel Department of the National Bank of Washington. I loved it. Steve adjusted. The girls learned to be responsible.

But I must admit, in the five years I worked at the bank, I never once let Steve's parents know that I had a paying job. It took a bit of finagling, but it was worth it to let my husband be the sole breadwinner in his father's eyes.

About this time in our life, Steve decided we needed to spice up our recipes. (He'd tried once before when we'd been married about six years—brought me a *just because* present of a three-inch-thick cookbook that featured a different recipe for every day of the year. I'd cried (definitely *not* in joy). I'd worried, *Now he's going to expect me to actually use this monstrosity. I'll spend the rest of my life in the kitchen!*

Now, a few more years of cooking under my belt, I began perusing *Better Homes and Gardens* for recipes. Brought deviled steak, country style cube-steak, baked chicken, and veal pie into our life. Got a new chicken recipe book and discovered Mornay chicken. (All these years later, all of us, Michele and Stephanie and Steve and I, still use all five of the recipes I first cooked so many years ago.)

We bought a Dutch oven (paid an outrageous $9.98 at Ernst Hardware) so we'd be ready when a recipe required one.

One Saturday, after he checked out the new *Sunset*, Steve gave me a grocery list for a gourmet stew—beef, vegetables, spices, and a very special (i.e. expensive) bottle of wine. I checked out two local markets to no avail—had to make a special trip to the liquor store.

That Sunday, Michele, Stephanie, and I sat down to dinner expecting something super.

"It's purple," Stephanie complained first thing. (And this is our daughter whose closet is always filled with shades of purple clothes.)

Michele made a face and said, "It smells funny."

Steve gave them *the look* and said, "*Eat!*"

We ate—we gagged—we filled up on vanilla ice cream and oatmeal cookies.

Ever since that meal, in our family, *Purple Stew* is the epitome of bad.

After a few years Steve got antsy. "I want to be on my own," he confided.

On his own? I agonized. *Like in not having a twice-a-month paycheck? No expense account?* But I didn't ask. I trusted him. *We won't be broke*, I assured myself. *I'll still have my job with the bank.*

"All I'm doing is selling life insurance," he complained.

"You just won another contest. The company sent us to Vancouver, British Columbia just last month. Heaven's sake, they put us up in the Bay Shore—top of the line."

Chapter 4

"I want to start my own independent insurance agency. It kills me to see the auto and homeowner's and commercial business that I can't write."

"Okay," I said meekly as I bit my tongue, trying not to let my worry show.

Steve began the process of going into business for himself by renting an office. He had good taste—it was in one of the newest, prime-location complexes in Lakewood. He used his head—got the space with the cheapest rent—on the second floor, with only a reception room, inside (windowless) office, and a teeny bathroom that doubled as a kitchen.

In his spare time (still working for the life company), he got appointments with two big A+ companies.

One day, Steve got an idea *out of the blue*. He stopped at a hole-in-the-wall insurance agency a couple of blocks away.

"I heard you're looking to sell your agency," Steve said.

"No," said the owner, Norm. (We later found that his *thing* was family counseling—he'd only got in the insurance business to *pay the bills*.)

"Well, if you change your mind, I'd appreciate it if you'd give me a call," Steve said.

Just a few days later, Norm showed up in our office, talked to Steve, and ended up selling his agency to us *on time*—three years of monthly payments.

It was a win-win business deal. Norm got to do what he was trained to do as a psychologist. And Steve got to build an insurance agency. Quick.

Norm loaned him the two file cabinets that housed his files, a desk, and two chairs.

That day—April 1, 1974—Steve gave notice, and Matule Insurance Center began.

Starting a business was scary. To me.

As an agent, I knew that Steve only got 17.5 percent of the premium. Out of that, he had to pay rent, utilities, office expenses, salaries, and loan payments—before he took a dime for himself.

For six weeks, Steve had our daughter Michele work at the office after she got out of high school. That gave him a couple of hours to get out and talk to prospective clients.

Finally, my husband sat me down to "talk." He had a strange look on his face.

"I need a fulltime person to answer the phone and make appointments for me. I'm losing business being tied to my desk."

Oh, oh! I thought. *Here it comes.*

"Why don't you come work with me? We'd be crazy to take your salary from the bank and use it to pay a secretary at the insurance office. How about it?"

I remembered the ten years my family owned a small motel—how hard we all had to work—the employee who stole money from us—the times business slowed and a bank note was due. I'd told myself, *Never me!*

Yet, Steve and I weren't my parents. Steve was full of enthusiasm for his new business. He'd proved he could sell insurance when he worked for top insurance companies. *It's Steve's time to shine*, I told myself.

Reluctantly, I said a quiet, "Okay."

The day I gave notice, I lost my balance while hurrying down a steep city pedestrian walk (an escalator without stairs) between Broadway and Pacific Avenue on my way to work. I kept going all day, walked four blocks to where I'd parked my car, drove home, and made dinner. At a quarter to eight, my friend Janet drove up our driveway and honked—we were going to our once-a-month girl's bridge party. Always fun.

My foot had hurt all day—not enough to go home—just enough to be bothersome. But sitting down—resting—playing cards, what began as a dull ache turned into full blown pain. I complained as I bid. "Four hearts."

Janet looked down and said, "Darlene, your leg is blowing up like a balloon!" Karen, the hostess of the evening, got me a chair to rest my leg on. I dragged it from one table to the other as we played bridge.

After a night of pain, I went to the doctor, had x-rays, and found that I'd broken several small bones in my right foot. "Not a big deal," the doctor said. "I can't even cast it. Just take it easy for a month or so, and you'll be good as new."

I spent my first month in the new Matule Insurance Center office hobbling up and down the stairs on crutches (no elevator).

Our office was just a couple of blocks from St. Frances Cabrini Church. I found myself making side trips there when I went to the bank (or any

Chapter 4

other excuse I could think of). Five minutes on my knees, three times a week kept me sane. I became very proficient with *petition* prayers. Looking back, I know I should have said *thank-you* a lot more.

As Steve found out, Norm only sold insurance to people who *needed* insurance. *Need to insurance your cars?*—He'd sell you a policy. *Need homeowner's insurance?*—He'd get it for you. But he never thought of selling an auto insurance customer a homeowners policy. *Besides.*

The beauty was that Steve could *cross sell*. Auto policies renew every six months. Homeowners every year. By April 1, 1975, Steve had sold almost every auto customer a homeowners—and visa-versa with homeowners. Commercials were bonuses.

At the end of the first year, we were well on our way to success.

We never even had to change our standard of living.

In June we visited Steve's family, and I admitted that I was working at the agency. *Finally I don't have to lead a double life!"*

"Thank God you never went to work for a bank or something shitty like that!" Steve's dad said. "I've got no use for those sons-a-bitches who put their wives to work."

I cringed—almost choked.

"But it's okay to work for your husband," he said. "That's different!"

The agency did well. We were on our way.

Steve and I became very active in the Lakewood business community.

Right after he opened his office, our vet friend, Max, invited Steve to join Rotary. The 110 members were the movers and shakers of Lakewood. Their annual Easter Pancake Breakfast netted over $25,000 that they spent on youth sports, education, and community service.

When a member died of renal failure at age thirty-seven, they decided to build a much-needed renal dialysis center at St. Joseph's hospital in Tacoma at a cost of several-hundred-thousand dollars. They funded it in a year-long project that culminated in a money-maker that featured a talk by the nationally acclaimed economist Milton Friedman at the Fifth Avenue Theater in Seattle. They had a full house.

Steve was a Rotary board member for years. He also acted as President of the Civil Service Commission for the Lakewood Fire Department.

Sixty Shades of Love

As a business owner, Steve belonged to the Lakewood Chamber of Commerce. Being a board member led to his election as president.

When the Villa Plaza shopping center looked like it might close, Steve went to Bellevue to meet with an investor (found they were both Gonzaga graduates) to interest him in buying the existing buildings, remodeling them, and adding several new anchor stores. They clicked. Steve ended up as a liaison between the Lakewood community and the new owner. We went to the gala opening—still have the complimentary champagne flutes they gave us.

As Chamber President, he also became an honorary colonel at McChord Air Force Base. (The McChord Commander was an honorary member of the Lakewood Chamber.)

During Steve's year as chamber executive, we were included in dozens of events at the airbase. One I remember fondly was when McChord hosted the Charleston, South Carolina Chamber of Commerce officers and their wives.

Another plus was becoming friends with the base chaplain, Father Kaz. We invited him to our home for holidays and to our condo in Lake Chelan Shores.

I've left the best for the last. McChord had what they called Business Leader Conferences at other bases in the country. Both Steve and I were invited to go.

Steve went twice, touring a total of three bases—Altus Air Force Base in Altus, Oklahoma, Kirtland in Albuquerque, New Mexico, and Scott, in Illinois, just outside St. Louis.

While I only went on one conference trip, I thoroughly enjoyed all aspects of the two bases I visited—Altus and Kirtland. At Altus, our group took a side trip to a cotton gin. And practiced flying in the cockpit of the base simulator (I crashed.) At Kirtland we were escorted into a top secret laboratory where we saw a demonstration of the (then) new possibilities of laser weapons. Flying back, I was invited into the cockpit twice—when the pilot guided the plane in a breathtaking sweep over the Grand Canyon and again as he flew over the crater that was once Mount St. Helens.

After we got back and shared experiences, Steve and I laughed when we both admitted to crashing the simulator into the main building at Altus. (And I had thought I was the only one!)

Chapter 4

I started my community service in Lakewood as a Girl Scout Leader and ended up president of several organizations: Lakewood Junior Women's Club, Lakewood Women of Rotary, Lakewood Women of Business, and board member of the Lakewood Library.

Both of us thrived.

Chapter 5

AFTER TEN YEARS IN our Emerald Drive home, we found acreage on nearby Chambers Creek and had a two-story Tudor custom home built—*creekside*.

The day we moved in, we hosted a dinner party that included our builder Leo, his carpenter, our friend/mover/helper Carl Luttinen, and their wives. What a celebration!

~

"Fire!" Steve shouted. "Get up!"

I opened my eyes. Saw Steve standing at the window. Flames were shooting up—right across the creek.

"Stromberg's house is on fire," he said. "It looks like the fire truck's just sitting on the bridge. I'm going to see what's the matter."

Before I knew it, my husband was gone.

"My God!" I gasped. "The whole valley could go!"

We lived in a forest. The cedar and Douglas fir trees were tall and thick. We'd just moved into our dream home—two weeks before.

I threw on some clothes and ran for the front door. At the stairs I stopped. Realized . . . *Stephanie's upstairs. Sound asleep.* I hurried upstairs. Woke her.

"Steph," I cried. "Get dressed! The neighbor's house is on fire. I'm going to see if I can help. Dad's gone already. You know where we'll be. Be careful."

Thank God she's almost sixteen! I knew she'd be fine.

I dashed outside and down to the bridge.

Steve was livid when I found him.

Chapter 5

"When I got here the firemen were just sitting in their truck. Like they were at the Red Sea waiting for Moses to part the water. Can you imagine? They asked, 'Will the bridge hold?'"

"Of course it will!" Steve said. "Don't you guys talk to each other? One of your crew drove this very truck over and back a couple of days ago. 'Testing' they told me. Get the hell over there and put that fire out!"

We ran toward the brilliant red sky, two houses away.

The house was completely aflame when we arrived. And the firemen weren't fighting the fire.

"What's going on?" Steve yelled.

"We gotta wait for the crew to connect the hose at the nearest hydrant. (We found later it was a mile away—up the hill.)

"Why don't you toss your submersible pump in the creek?"

"The water's pretty fast. It might get away from us."

"For Christ's sake," Steve yelled. "I'll jump in myself and hold it steady!"

Just then we saw Bill Stromberg dragging his wife Pauline out of the garage.

Thank goodness! They're alive! I rejoiced.

Both were barefooted. I saw Pauline shivering in her nightgown. Bill wore only a pair of pants.

About that time Caesar and Fran DeVita arrived from next door. Seeing the situation, Fran ran home to get some clothes for Bill and Pauline. Caesar began hosing the side of his house.

Steve and I tried to calm the Strombergs. They were dazed.

Finally, the hose arrived, and the fireman began spraying water on the inferno. Nothing stopped the flames.

"It's the cedar," Bill agonized. "I wanted an all-cedar house—siding, shake roof, cedar planks instead of sheetrock." He choked. "I might as well have signed my own death warrant."

Fran and I got Pauline to the DeVitas' house. Got her to sit down—sip some coffee. We were all numb by that time. Yet, if the wind came up, we still had the worry of the fire igniting the trees and burning the other thirteen homes on Chambers Creek Lane.

Ann and Norm Tremaine from next door joined us. Our Stephanie dropped by and drank her first-ever (she told us later) cup of coffee.

About that time Fran's daughter, who was visiting with her four-year-old, ran down the stairs saying, "I'm ready to go." We all gasped. All she was carrying was her makeup case. She'd forgotten her little girl upstairs, sound asleep.

We waited—for what seemed forever. The fire—so huge it was sighted in the night sky five miles away at the Narrows Bridge—was finally contained.

We all breathed a sigh of relief.

⌒

But—there was a problem—with Bill's homeowners insurance.

No—the company didn't refuse to pay the damages. The cause was determined quickly—an instant-on TV. Companies typically would rather pay for one total than a single policy with a half-dozen small claims.

But the fact was—the house wasn't insured for replacement cost.

When Bill had come into our insurance agency to have Steve write his homeowner's insurance—two weeks before the fire—Steve figured out the replacement cost. Bill declined. "Too high," he said. "I built that house myself. It didn't cost me anywhere near that much." So Steve used the lower amount Bill wanted.

When it came time to rebuild, Bill was $50,000 dollars short. Thank goodness he was pragmatic.

Bill did rebuild it—by himself. It took him a year-and-a-half. For all that time he and Pauline lived in a twelve-foot travel trailer.

Funny thing—the fire forged a strong bond between us and the three families who lived directly across the creek—one only severed by death.

Because of this experience, Steve changed his whole approach in selling homeowners insurance. If, after he explained replacement coverage to a potential client, they said, *Don't need it*, he'd say, "Let me tell you about a man named Bill . . .

Over the years only a handful of people declined after hearing Steve's story. To those he politely said, "Sorry, I think you need another agent. I can't sleep nights if I don't do the best for my clients."

⌒

Our first year on the creek, Christmas began in September. At least for me.

In those days, fabric shops didn't have the variety of holiday fabrics they do now. I began searching for appropriate combinations for the new holiday stockings I planned to make.

Chapter 5

My final choices were two red—Steve's a red and white stripe and Stephanie's a big print—and two green—Michele's green and white polka dots, mine checks. Each stocking was eighteen inches long. I *couched* each person's name in cursive using red or green narrow braid on the white pique cuffs.

In the years since, I've made and displayed many other stockings—for my mother, various animals, sons-in-law, and (beginning in the year of their birth) three grandsons. Our mantle was pretty crowded for a while. Now we're down to daughters, grandsons, and Steve and me.

I could spend months and reams of paper listing all the handmade ornaments I made—fabric ones (from ginger-bread men to candy canes), tole-painted (from Mr. and Mrs. Santa Claus to angels to Raggedy Ann and Andy miniatures). *But I've got to get this story moving.*

As Christmas got closer, both Steve and I realized that something from the past wasn't right for the present—our Christmas Castle. It was just too small.

First we decided to move it from underneath the tree to sit on the biggest under-used spot we had—my mother's big cedar chest. We used every inch of that space.

Steve got right on the project—we always decorated the house for the holidays the weekend after Thanksgiving. It was already almost Halloween.

He changed his mode of construction on the turrets. This time he got four larger carpet spools—the kind with metal end caps. This gave them more body and changed the building slightly, the roofs being flat.

After two undercoats of paint, Steve stuccoed the outside with spackle. I papered the inside walls with textured white wallpaper.

I found some large red glass *diamonds* at a stained glass shop and added them to the turrets.

Steve's next step turned our castle from one belonging to a minor prince to that of a king. By cutting tongue depressors into pieces, gluing them down, and staining the finished product walnut, he created a gleaming parquet floor.

"What our castle needs is a moat to finish it off," Steve said.

We found a long, slim mirror and put it directly in front of the entrance—an instant moat. Steve made a draw bridge from the wood he'd cut out for the castle entrance. As a finishing touch Steve attached gold chains on each side so the king could close up the castle in case of attack.

Outside, we added evergreen trees and two soldiers at guard over the gate. Inside, I placed the miniature furniture from the first castle, and more soldiers on the mezzanine.

―

The wonderful friends who came to our Christmas brunches often gave us wooden gift boxes filled with wine bottles. The quality of the wood was so good that it literally hurt to put them in the trash.

"Why don't we make something creative?" Steve suggested.

"I'd love somewhere to display the miniatures I've been collecting," I said.

Thus began our first Alpine chalet. We ended up with a total of five. And I begin searching for more items to display.

―

One year I surprised Steve with a model train. (He'd always wanted one as a little boy—had always been disappointed.) He decided to put it on a permanent track (round of plywood covered by white felt to give the illusion of snow) big enough to use under our Christmas tree.

We decided to turn the center into a miniature town with houses, a train depot (for Steve's new toy), a fabric shop (for me to buy even more Christmas fabric). And village people galore. It was fun watching the train go round and round as we enjoyed our holiday trimmings.

―

One of my all-time favorite Christmas projects is my only trapunto.

Trapunto is the Italian word meaning *to quilt*. Since I'd moved to Lakewood, I'd already made four bedspreads using regular quilting procedure. When I heard a local shop was giving lessons in this specialty method, I convinced my daughter Michele to go to a trapunto class with me. I was fascinated. Being November, the fabric store had lengths of Finnish fabric depicting a Christmas scene at an old-country train depot.

"Perfect!" I said as I gave the clerk my $10.00.

The process was simple. I placed a piece of batting between the printed material and a lining. Then I outlined items I wanted to emphasize—small

Chapter 5

and large. In the background I fashioned rows of snow drifts and outlined some evergreen trees. The train almost jumped off the material on the foreground. For the finale, I created a three-inch *frame* from red velvet, sewed it around the quilted fabric, and fastened the *picture* to a wood frame.

The finished trapunto piece was splashy and colorful, big enough to place on the mantle of my floor-to-cathedral-ceiling massive stone fireplace. It was the first thing guests saw when entering our family room.

And last, but definitely not least, was my cone wreath. If time were money, I could *not* have afforded it.

My friend Janet provided the instructions—take a few pinecones (free in the nearby woods), some wire and green floral tape (cost negligible), and a circle of plywood (Karen's husband had some leftover wood that he offered to donate and cut into the specific size), and follow directions (we were all intelligent and nimble fingered). *A piece of cake*, we all agreed.

Besides it gave us an excuse to get together. We decided to meet one evening a month. Because the frames were bulky (three-foot diameter—a 36-inch wooden circle) and Karen's garage had the most storage space, she volunteered to host the group. We took turns providing wine. (Wreath-making creates a healthy thirst.)

The first night we divided and began wrapping the wires. The second month we got so animated over some earth-shaking event (I would supply information, but it has somehow disappeared from my memory) that we never quite got down to working.

I'm not quite sure if we got done with the hardware aspect of our project the third session, but I'm pretty sure we got close.

We had to develop the knack of attaching the wires to both the frame and the cones, being sure to hide them. By June we'd gotten a good start. We decided to take July and August off to allow for family vacations.

By the next June, we'd made real progress. "We'll have our wreaths finished for the coming Christmas," we prophesied. We were nowhere close to finishing by that Christmas. In fact we weren't done by the next.

Karen asked, "Don't some of the places look a little *light*."

I took a good look. Agreed. Janet rolled her eyes and poured us each another glass of wine. We decided to buy some sugar pines, and learned how to cut them creatively.

Perhaps the reason for our slow delivery was simple—we had a lot to talk about. We each had a husband. Janet had four kids, Karen three, and I had two. We were friends when we began. By the time we finished, we were bosom buddies.

I have to brag, our completed wreaths were creations of beauty. I know I treasured mine.

By the time we'd finished our long-time project, Steve and I'd moved to our creek house a mile away. But our friendship had been sealed.

And the Matule annual Christmas brunch tradition lasted for thirty happy years.

I had a twenty-year love affair with Chambers Creek.

Steve and I poured our all into our Creek place. We helped the builder design the floor plan. We did all the interior painting and wallpapering. We spent our first summer—Memorial Day to Labor Day—clearing the half-lot next to our original property.

We loved the showplace garden that evolved—rhododendrons, azaleas, hydrangeas—even called our favorite rhodys by name. My favorite was Cynthia. Steve's was Sappho.

As fall approached I said, "It's going to start raining soon. How are we going to get all our yard work done?" Steve gave me one of his *trust-me* grins, dug in the mail, and produced the new *Land's End* catalog. "See," he said as he pointed to bright yellow *his-and-hers* slickers.

I saw. Agreed. Ordered.

That September, after driving Michele to Pomona College in Claremont, California and checking out the college, Steve drove north to Santa Barbara. I was teary most of the way—knowing I wouldn't see my seventeen-year-old daughter until Christmas.

But he found an Italian restaurant on the ocean, and we enjoyed a romantic meal. And each other.

The next day we followed the Coast Highway—saw some breathtaking scenery. We toured San Simeon, oohed and ahhed at the opulence, and giggled at the tiny beds these more-than-rich people slept in. Carmel Mission was a disappointment. The day we arrived everything was closed to the

Chapter 5

public. We made do with a ride by Pebble Beach Golf Course, and stayed in Monterey that night.

Getting up at dawn the next morning, we drove to our next destination—San Francisco. I fully intended to leave my heart there. What a day we had! We cruised the shops at the waterfront. I drooled as I tested the chocolate—dreamed of ball dresses as I fondled the silk fabric—stopped in my tracks as I gazed into an art gallery.

The colors! I thought as I stood on the street looking in. *Just the shades I've chosen for my new living room.* I hurried in, dragging Steve inside with me.

Inside, the greens and rusts paled when I saw the little girl in the oil painting. She looked just like my daughters at age five—ready to begin kindergarten—decked out in their smock-like dress (they both wore the same one the first day).

In a tall and narrow frame, the little girl stood sideways, holding a Raggedy Ann doll. I felt a tear of memory leaking from my heart.

"Look at this one," Steve said drawing my attention to a smaller painting. "It looks like both of the girls. One with blond hair—the other a little darker."

It was smaller than the first picture, but had the same color scheme. I loved the distinctive octagon frame... In my mind's eye, I saw *both* pictures on my wall.

Then I checked the price. Gasped. I dragged Steve outside, muttering, "Too much money! Too much."

"It's lunch time," he said, changing the subject. We ate seafood while watching boats sail back and forth on the Pacific blue water of San Francisco Bay.

Gump's was our afternoon destination. For a girl who got her china and sterling at the tiny Bowles Jewelry in Glasgow, Montana (I registered my choices there), Gump's china and silver overwhelmed me. I'd thought that the Crescent in Spokane and Frederick and Nelson in Seattle had the epitome of variety. No more! Gump's was more like a museum than a department store. We enjoyed a mini-tour of exotic Orient—Jade—a bigger-than-life bronze Buddha—porcelains and silks.

That night we ate at DiMaggio's and went to bed exhausted.

First thing in the morning, Steve said, "We're going back and buy those paintings. I don't care how much they cost." I didn't argue too much.

For lunch, Steve insisted on taking me to the Top of the Mark in Nob Hill (he'd been there on a business trip and had vowed to treat me as soon as he could). The view encompassed a 360-degree scan of the city. I love roof-top restaurants.

The meal was delicious—the service perfect.

"Magic," I proclaimed in wonder.

After lunch we walked through downtown. I stopped at I. Magnin's, but didn't suggest going in. Steve didn't insist (guess he realized it was ultra-expensive), but he did say, "You've got to get an outfit to remember this trip." I ended up with two sweaters from Macy's—one winter-white and one petal-pink. I wore them for years—remembering our San Francisco sojourn every time—what a beautiful memory!

It was almost 9 p.m. before we reached Redding. We stopped at the first nice-looking motel we found with an adjoining restaurant.

While waiting for our T-bone steaks, we sipped Manhattans—two each if I remember—and savored our perfect day.

But, as we found out soon, the day was far from over. We loved each other that night with an indescribable depth—a lasting joy.

Forever since, our benchmark for *perfect* has been—and is—*Redding*.

Chambers Creek was a spiritual place. Just after Steve and I celebrated our Twentieth Wedding Anniversary, we were inspired to go to a weekend Marriage Encounter. Recently I found this memory in the notebook I'd saved . . .

Dearest Steve,

Being married to you is the best thing that's ever happened to me!

Sometimes it's a comfortable feeling, like being able to snuggle up while we're watching TV. Sometimes it's another kind of comfortable—like when you really understand when my mother upsets me.

Sometimes it's exciting like when we make love. Marriage Encounter has been an aphrodisiac.

Being married to you has given me my childhood dream—a gorgeous house—which I would never have had without you. It's not everyone whose dreams come true.

Chapter 5

Being married to you is an adventure. It makes me feel like Columbus when I discover new things about you. (And I thought I knew you so well.)

Being married to you is not exactly what I expected. I never expected to pull weeds and balance the check book. However, I never expected to buy two original oil paintings at a shop in San Francisco, and then have lunch at the Top of the Mark. And—that evening—to have a momentous second honeymoon night in Redding.

Being married to you makes me feel like a different person than I had been twenty years ago.

Thank you.
Love,

Me

Chapter 6

ONE RAINY NOVEMBER DAY, Steve got a surprise phone call from his sister, Dodo. Recently divorced and the single mother of three kids ages six, seven, and nine, she got minimal help from her ex and didn't have the money for daytime long-distance phone calls.

"The doctor told me I need surgery," she said. "Right away."

I could hear the fear in her voice from where I was sitting—across from Steve.

"Is Mom coming?" he asked.

"No, you know her. She won't even go the thirty miles to Anaconda. Minnesota is definitely out of the picture."

"What did Sis say?"

A pause. Then Dodo said, "No. She's busy."

"Let me talk to her," I said. I didn't have to say it twice. Steve and I often finished each other's sentences, and we were both on the same wave length on this.

"Would you like me to fly over?" I asked Dodo.

I've never *heard* relief before, but I definitely did that day.

We quickly made plans.

Our insurance agency was new. Since I *did the books*, there was a lot to do—I'd be gone two weeks. But I wasn't worried about leaving Steve at home alone with Stephanie. She was sixteen and knew how to clean and help cook. They'd do fine.

An only child, I'd adopted Dodo as my kid sister. And helping family was very important to me.

Dodo met me at the Minneapolis airport with her friend, Linda. The kids, Wendi, John, and Steve, were at school. By noon, we were up north at Dodo's house in Coon Rapids where she showed me the ropes. When the

Chapter 6

kids returned from school, Linda drove us all to St. Paul where we got Dodo settled in the hospital.

When we got ready to leave, the boys were stoic—Wendi cried. It was hard for them to say goodbye to their Mom—even if their Auntie Darlene would be living with them. Dodo was her children's rock.

It wasn't like the kids and I weren't acquainted. When Stephanie was eight and Michele eleven, the four of us had made a trip from Tacoma to Minneapolis with stops off at the Black Hills and my Aunt Inga and Uncle Sander's farm just outside of Fargo, North Dakota. My nephew Steve was a baby during that visit.

We'd often met in Butte over the years. Just the previous summer Dodo, and her three kids had driven from Butte to our home on Chamber's Creek where they'd stayed a couple of days.

The first night the kids must have been tired. Everyone went to sleep without a fuss.

I was worn out and went to bed at 8:30 Tacoma time. Not like me!

The next morning the alarm didn't go off. Even though I had to hurry to get the kids ready, I made sure I sent them off to school with hugs and full tummies.

Linda arrived soon after, and the two of us went to the hospital. We stayed with Dodo until the nurse took her to surgery.

I got back by 1 p.m. and had a batch of oatmeal cookies warm and just out of the oven when my three charges got home from school. The cookies were a hit.

For dinner I served baked ham. Not knowing Steve *hated* ham, I gave him the biggest piece. I found *that* out quickly.

"Auntie Darlene may I get some barbecue sauce from the refrigerator?" he asked.

"Sure," I replied—curious. I got the picture when he doused the meat with barbecue sauce. But he never complained and ate every bite.

The phone rang when we were clearing the table. "I just talked to Dodo," Linda said. "The surgery was a complete success. She's a bit groggy but would love to see her gang. I know I said I couldn't drive you back and forth to the hospital every day, but I don't want your first solo run to be in the dark. Could you be ready in ten minutes?"

The four of us hurried doing the dishes and were ready nine minutes later when Linda drove up the driveway and honked her horn.

Dodo was in great spirits when she saw her trio rush in.

"Be careful," I told them. "Your mom had stitches." They all understood stitches.

I saw her flinch once. But each one—Steve and John and Wendi—got their hug. The grins on three little faces—and on a happy mom—attested to the warmth of their love.

The next morning I got the three off to school with full intention of working on a new novel I was writing. I hadn't even gotten all my supplies out before I heard an insistent bell ringing. I rushed to the front door—and found John.

"My tummy hurts," he said. I gave him a keen look and took his temperature holding my right hand on his forehead (I could tell this was serious!). Nurse Darlene healed him with the miracle medicines of tea and a stick of Dentyne gum.

That day I was scheduled to drive the thirty-five miles—each way—to the hospital by myself for the first time. With John in the navigator seat and a Twin Cities map between us, we set off. He was a great conversationalist.

Dodo was surprised. John shone as an only child.

On the way back, I missed the turn north and found myself on a highway that said, *Duluth ahead*. We took a good twenty-mile detour. On the way back I spied a Bridgeman's Ice Cream store.

"Hungry?" I asked.

"One scoop or two?" he asked.

"I'm having a cherry milkshake. Want one too?" His eyes lit up as he nodded.

"You know, John," I said between sips, "we can't have adventures like this every day. In fact I think today should be our secret."

"I like secrets," he assured me.

Dodo's kids were well trained. They all had their chores and did them without being told. But the second night I found out that boys were definitely different than girls to raise. I'd thought my girls fought. *Wrong.* They just

Chapter 6

had spirited discussions. Steve and John shared a bedroom and had fist fights. They yelled.

I floundered before I negotiated a truce. Result—I went to bed worn out.

On Day Four, I almost didn't make it to the hospital. When I pulled down the garage door, I lost control. It banged down. Three fingers ended up in a vise grip between the edge of the door and the cement floor. There I was in the middle of an empty neighborhood. Everyone was at work.

What can I do? I tried a quick prayer. And, either it worked, or my fingers got paper thin by magic. I pulled. Felt pain. But got loose.

Dodo was looking good when I finally got to her room. "The doctor is letting me go home tomorrow."

We shared a celebratory hug.

The next day I changed three beds, vacuumed the whole house, and scrubbed the kitchen and bathroom. You'd have thought I was getting company.

Dodo was excited to leave the hospital, and we had a good *girl talk* on the way back to Coon Rapids.

While Dodo napped, I made spaghetti and meatballs. While all was quiet, I called my Aunt Minnie who lived in St. Paul. We had a good visit.

That night I taught John how to play rummy and played individual games with Steve, John, and Wendi.

After putting the kids to bed, Dodo and I celebrated her homecoming with a bottle of sparkling wine. I remember complimenting her—"Your kids are great!"

She demurred and said, "Well—they have their moments."

"No, I mean it. You can tell there's a lot of love in this house." That led to talk about how life was in the Matule house when she and Steve were kids.

"Steve always said things were *so* much better after you were born (there's an eleven year gap in their ages)."

"You've got to be kidding," she said. "There wasn't *any* happiness in our house when I was growing up. Or *real* communication. In fact, my best memories of those days are all focused on Steve. I loved the summers I got to spend with you guys in Spokane."

The next week, after the kids went to bed, Dodo and I sat up every night until the wee hours—talking about life. We became friends, not just sisters-in-law.

At my insistence, Dodo took a home vacation while she recuperated.

I got the kids off to school every day, cooked all the meals, cleaned the house, did the laundry, and shopped for groceries. One day I took Dodo to the shopping center so she could get some necessities. We had lunch at the Fox and Hounds, a supper club where she worked as office manager.

I got the kids to the dentist and swimming lessons. Took them to church on Sunday and afterwards to a nice restaurant for brunch. Watched movies on TV. Enjoyed interacting with them.

But I took personal time too. My father had just died the previous February and left me with lots of questions about his family. (I'd been told he'd been orphaned at age eleven—but no details.) I'd been chasing leads ever since.

One day I drove down to St. Paul and had lunch with Daddy's sister Minnie and her husband Uncle Ray. After we got comfortable with each other, I asked my aunt how my grandmother died.

"Oh, she got run over by a horse," Minnie said.

Uncle Ray rolled his eyes and said, "Well, that's the first time I've heard *that* story!"

There was total silence for what seemed like forever. Then they both started talking at the same time. The *remembering* stopped.

I left with more questions than I'd had when I got there.

I'd written to my cousin Arlin (his mother was Daddy's sister Inga) who lived across the state, almost to Fargo, North Dakota. *I'd love for us to get together while I'm in Coon Rapids*, I wrote. *How about flying over one afternoon?"* (I knew he had a small Cessna he used in his John Deere business.) He jumped at the chance.

One afternoon I picked Arlin up at the local small airport at 4:30. We spent five hours visiting and eating at the Smuggler's Inn. (I'm surprised we weren't asked to leave—figured he left a big tip.)

Arlin was as interested in finding out our family history as I was. We shared each other's information. I told him what Minnie had just revealed.

Chapter 6

"Wow," he exclaimed. "I never heard that story before either. I'm going to grill my mother about her memories. I know she remembers a lot. But, as you know, the Barnes family is *very* secretive."

We both promised to keep working at finding our *roots*. And to keep in contact.

My last personal trip was to St. Paul. Daddy's cousin Olga invited me for lunch at her home. She told me stories of having my grandfather live with her family when she was a preschooler. What he looked like. I felt like I'd won the lottery.

On my last day at Dodo's, I got the house spic-and-span and did the laundry. Knowing how the kids loved sweets, I baked up a storm (filled two big coffee cans with oatmeal cookies to freeze—and the cookie jar on the kitchen counter). Our final dinner together was broiled pork chops—their favorite. Everyone cleaned their plate.

As I spent a final evening with Dodo, Steve, John, and Wendi, I realized how much I actually hated to leave. I'd come to really *know* each one and love them all as if they were my own progeny.

Over the years, we've all stayed close. I can't imagine having missed those very special weeks. I feel blessed.

Chapter 7

THE NEXT JUNE, STEVE and I drove to Lake Chelan to attend the Big I (Independent Insurance Agents) annual meeting. Steve planned to earn the continuing education credits he needed and catch up with his friends. I went for a mini-vacation—I had two good books in my suitcase.

I hadn't told Steve I'd visited Chelan in 1954.

One October Saturday that fall I'd gone with my then boyfriend Mike and his mother for the day. We had lunch with some old friends of hers who lived on one of the apple orchards.

That afternoon Mike showed me all his haunts from the two years he'd gone to Chelan High School, 1950-52. It was a sleepy little town—much like Glasgow. The town jeweler even had his shop in the exact same location as Baker Jewelry in my home town. I was back in my dorm before 10 p.m.

By the time Steve and I arrived in Chelan, and I began having déjà vu feelings, it seemed too late to mention my earlier visit.

I oohed and ahhed at the beauty of the lake and Chelan Butte in unison with Steve. Yet, as we drove north to the resort at Wapato Point, I kept having the feeling, *There's something special here for me.*

About halfway from the City of Chelan to Manson, we saw a big sign that said:

New Condos—Pick Yours Today

After the meetings were over the first day, Steve and I drove down and toured the cream-colored, two-story stucco buildings with red tile roofs.

We both fell in love with Lake Chelan Shores on the spot.

Chapter 7

I had an extra dimension to my feelings. It was as if I'd finally come home. Home to a peaceful place I'd been looking for since I'd first seen it almost twenty years before.

Synchronicity had once again manifested itself in my life.

The next day we returned and chose Unit 8-8. On the second floor, our place had a bedroom, bath, kitchen, and living room on the main floor—and a second bedroom in the loft. For a $500 earnest money payment, we were the proud owners (well, almost) of eight weeks a year—two weeks in each season—of a luxurious condominium.

As I remember that day in 1980, all these years later, I can't help but look at Steve and me with *now* eyes.

We'd begun that March by paying the last check for Michele's Pomona College four-year education (no student loans for *our* daughter) and flying to Hawaii for our first tropical holiday. We'd just bought a vacation condo, and were preparing for a three week trip to Dubrovnik, Yugoslavia in September.

Those were the days when Steve and I were *rich and didn't know it.*

Sadly, I realize we didn't appreciate our good fortune. How I wish we'd taken the time to look upwards and say, "Thank you, Lord."

But oh, how we enjoyed our time at Lake Chelan Shores!

In the twenty years we had our condo, we seldom missed using our designated weeks. We invited friends—Sandy and Carl Luttinen liked it so much that they still own their four-week-a-year share. Bert and George Barrett came from Charlotte, North Carolina.

I still remember the spring day Sandy and I strolled the grounds bemoaning our lack of grandchildren. (Both of our daughters had been married for several years with no sign of a single baby.) Lo and behold, we both had grandsons—eight months later—one week apart. I still treasure a picture of the two new moms and their babies at the Lake Chelan pool the next summer.

Our daughters visited—with friends and husbands. Our grandkids came—a special time always!

When the boys rode over with us, we always played a game as we approached town. The first to say, "I see the lake" would get a prize. Granted the winner got the *first* chance to pick his toy at the variety store in town, but we always got the other guy *something*. Chelan meant fun!

One of my favorite things was taking Larry and Sean outside when it got dark. The stars are spectacular in Chelan—away from city lights. It's like being in the middle of the Milky Way.

Their little eyes would be wide with wonder. I'd point out the Big Dipper and Cassiopeia (the only constellations I could label) and say:

> *Twinkle, twinkle, little star.*
> *How I wonder what you are.*
> *Up above the world so high,*
> *Like a diamond in the sky.*
> *Twinkle, twinkle, little star.*
> *How I wonder what you are.*

Then I'd tell them to close their eyes and make a wish. They'd squish up their little eyes, take a big breath, and make their wish. You could almost see their minds working.

It's one of the best memories this proud Nanny has of her boys!

For years I bought our daughter's birthday presents at Clampitt's—pretty dresses they always loved.

But perhaps the most memorable item we ever bought in Chelan was a library table. We were in the process of furnishing Steve's office in a colonial décor. After scouring all the antique stores, we found the perfect one in Manson. Bought it. Problem was—they didn't deliver. It certainly didn't fit in our Town Car!

Carl to the rescue. "We'll just put it in our boat when we leave on Friday and drive it home for you.

Problem was—Carl's home was on Bainbridge Island, and we lived on Chambers Creek—probably eighty miles away.

Another mutual friend joined the relay. Bill Taylor and Carl moved it to Bill's pickup, and he drove it right to the new office.

While I know furniture is just stuff, I loved that table. It was a sad day when we finally had to give it away when we down-sized to move to Brown's

Chapter 7

Point. Thank goodness I can *visit* it—a Wenatchee friend now uses it as her desk.

⌒

Steve's presence was definitely more important at our insurance agency than mine. So often, when our fall week came in October, I'd spend the week there by myself.

I loved those weeks. Alone. With myself—and my God.

I gazed onto the lake—ablaze with shimmering diamonds—and breathed in the wonders of nature being heaped at my feet.

Peace enveloped me as my eyes rose to *My Valley*—where the mountains parted and eternity seemed to beckon me.

I had a routine. Rise at seven, eat, drive to town, and go to Mass. Return to my typewriter and write, write, write. One memorable trip I finished one of my favorite chapters of my first novel, *Under the Gallus Frame*—when Tony, a main character, is dropped into Croatia in the middle of WWII.

I treated myself to dinner at Campbell's Friday evening—cooked whatever I wanted the other six nights (always had oyster stew and a sliced tomato one evening)—never missed having ice cream for dessert. I exercised after lunch, luxuriated in the hot tub afterwards, and wrote until *wine-time* at five when I'd sit on the patio and just *think*.

An hour of TV after dinner (one night I saw one of Stephanie's friends win a million-dollar lottery on the news), more writing, and then reading until 11:00.

Twice my dear friend, Phyllis Moen Sanguine, joined me. Having known each other since seventh grade, we shared secrets and talked about old times. Laughed a lot. Once cried. Special.

One October Thursday as I sat on the sofa looking out to the lake and *My Valley*, sipping a glass of wine, it started to snow. It snowed and snowed and snowed.

When I woke up on Friday it was still snowing.

I thought, *My God, I have to check out by noon. There are two passes between Chelan and home. What should I do?*

At ten I loaded the car and left. The road to Chelan and Highway Two were both clear, but plowing hadn't been started on the road up Blewett Pass. I waited on the side of the road for a few minutes until I saw a big semi coming. Got right behind him and followed his rig up and down the mountain.

"Whew!" I said when I got down. I stopped at Cle Elum, bought a cup of coffee (unknown for me—this was my milkshake diner) and a hamburger.

Snoqualmie Pass was much worse. Ice in places. Cars spun off the road everywhere. I kept a slow—very slow—pace up to the summit and back down to North Bend, where I treated myself to a cup of hot tea at McDonald's.

"You surprised me," Steve said when I arrived home at 5:30. "I kept waiting for a call from you saying you wanted me to come over and drive you home."

I glowed in my accomplishment.

Steve and I *second honeymooned* many times at our Chelan condo—sometimes just for a long weekend (depart Lakewood right after his noon Rotary meeting on Friday, get up before dawn on Monday, and arrive at the office by 8 a.m.) But we liked it best when we could stay the whole week—alone together. Neither of us was ever ready to leave.

One day Steve asked, "How long do you think it would take before you were ready to pack up and go home?" (I *had* said a three week stay in Hawaii was enough.)

I didn't answer immediately. Finally, I said, "Never. Absolutely never."

Of course, life happened. *Never* arrived.

Chapter 8

IT WAS 1981—A TYPICAL sunny August day.

Steve blindfolded me as I walked in the back door.

What in the world is my husband doing now? I wondered.

Gently he guided me up the back stairs toward the TV room. At the top he turned me, loosened the cloth that covered my eyes, pulled it aside, and said, "Happy Anniversary!"

Before me stood a miniature sailing ship—the *True Love* we'd both enjoyed on our honeymoon.

At that very moment Bing Crosby appeared on our big screen TV singing.

Our song.

Our moment!

Bless my dear husband Steve for creating such a beautiful tribute to our many years of love.

Champagne toasts followed as did a sumptuous dinner at one of my favorite places—E. R. Rogers in nearby Steilacoom.

The mystic of *True Love* began on our honeymoon when we first saw the movie in a tiny theater in Polson, Montana. Steve kept singing it as we drove around western Montana and over to our new home in Spokane. It always *put us in the mood.*

It probably helped that Grace Kelly, the female lead, had gotten married in a fairy tale marriage just months before Steve and I said our vows. It made us feel strangely connected.

In the early years of our marriage, we had to get by with hearing *True Love* sung on TV specials or the radio. But as soon as the movie *High Society* went on sale for home view we got a copy.

Watching Bing and Grace float over the screen became an event we still celebrate annually during our anniversary week. We pop in our disc (we're on at least the third copy) and for almost two hours we're transported to the magic of young love in the opulence of Westport. Bing and Sinatra both croon love songs to Grace and the two baritones delight us in their duo, "Well Did You Evah."

I imagine myself in Grace's elegant layered chiffon dresses (thank you genius of costuming, Helen Rose).

Steve mimics Grace as she enters the patio dressed in her wedding dress, puts her fingers over her eyes like an eyeshade, and asks, while seeming to be fighting a champagne headache, "Where *is* everybody?"

We giggle. Hold hands. Cuddle. Rejoice in our enduring love.

The original sailboat didn't last. Steve kept looking for a bigger, more professional craft. A few years ago, when we were celebrating yet another anniversary at Ocean Shores on the Washington coast, we found one at the gift shop of one of our favorite places on the Pacific, Ocean Crest Resort. The first thing we did when we got our new sailboat home was to christen it with a brass nameplate that says it all.

True Love—8-18-56.

༄

Our life overflowed with fun things.

We had season tickets to the Seahawks games—four—we always invited two guests. Steve knew that I wasn't crazy about football, so he made a day of it for us. We'd go to 8 a.m. Mass, and then pick up our guests and head north. Along the way we'd have brunch. After the game we'd stop for dinner.

What wasn't to like? I told myself. (I even learned, under Steve's tutelage, the basics of football and found it interesting.)

Then there was *my thing*—season tickets to the Fifth Avenue Theater in Seattle. I loved it! We were scheduled on Saturday night—five different plays a year—five days to enjoy Seattle.

Most of the presentations were musicals—*Annie, Pirates of Penzance, Seven Brides for Seven Brothers*—but it's a drama that I remember most. The reason? Because it starred Katherine Hepburn. She was unforgettable—I can't remember the name of the play!

Chapter 8

We began our theater trips by driving to Seattle in time for lunch. We'd shop, have dinner, and go to the play. Then Steve got the idea, "How'd you like to spend Saturday in the city and go home on Sunday?"

My eyes lit up.

First we spent one night at The Westin. Then Steve joined the WAC (Washington Athletic Club) where members could book a night's stay for a very reasonable amount. A plus was their dining room where they served gourmet cuisine.

My cup was full.

⁓

Views on smoking changed over the last sixty years. In the fifties, smoking was considered sophisticated.

I came to college having smoked one-third of one cigarette. (Phyllis and I had tried one in the restroom of the Orpheum Theatre in Glasgow one evening when we were bored.)

But I had a *shoe thing* that cost me money. I decided I couldn't afford the quarter a pack of smokes cost *and* all the pretty shoes that were saying, "Please, buy me."

Steve smoked.

I remember we were at the Gonzaga COG one Sunday watching a movie, and Steve offered me a lighted cigarette. I held it. Put it to my lips. Played with the smoke in my mouth for a few minutes. Decided it didn't taste good. Quit cold turkey.

When we got married, I remember going around the house sniffing. I'd ask Steve, "Don't the drapes smell funny?" He obliges me. Smells the curtains. Says, "It's in your head."

Pretty soon I quit asking because I didn't smell anything bad—smoke had become normal.

Twenty years later, Steve's doctor casually asked, "Have you ever considered quitting smoking?"

Then the Surgeon General delivered his report. Soon it was, "Steve, you *need* to quit smoking."

So Steve tried. He became a champion quitter. I'm sure he had the Guinness Book of Records prize.

I tried not to nag. I had Coit (top local carpet, drape, and upholstery cleaners) do the drapes regularly.

One day after his regular checkup Steve said, "The doctor suggested a sure way to quit smoking—choose a special event and tell everyone about your decision. So I've decided. I'm giving you a *smoke-free* husband for your birthday present."

I was excited! With that to look forward to I could hardly wait to be a year older.

The day came. Steve threw his cigarettes in the garbage—put all the ashtrays away *for company*—went around looking smug.

Three days later I found him smoking.

In all our years of marriage, I have never been angrier at my husband. I yelled. I was *not* nice!

Eight months later we went to a wedding reception at the Tacoma Country Club. Now I must tell you, Steve and I both sometimes socialize separately at these types of celebrations. So I wasn't surprised when I lost track of him.

What did shock me was to find Steve and an unknown lady hovering next to an over-flowing single ashtray. Apparently it was the only one in the whole building. My husband Steve looked sheepish—he knew how I felt about his smoking. I tried not to look smug.

The next Thursday I had a tough day at work and left later than usual. I grumbled to myself as I stopped at the grocery story to do my weekly shopping. It was raining. By the time I came out with a full grocery cart, it was pouring. The windshield wipers could barely cope with the deluge.

When I got home, Steve helped me unload the groceries. He peeked in a couple of sacks and asked, "Where are the cigarettes?"

"You never told me you were out," I said. "It's raining. And I'm tired. I'm *not* going back tonight."

To my surprise, I got no complaint. Calm as could be, Steve said, "Well, I'm not going either."

He never smoked another cigarette. He never bemoaned his loss. Not even once.

Soon a new Steve evolved—a non-smoking fanatic.

He threw out all the ashtrays at the office. He had a sign made and plopped it slap-dab in the middle of his desk. Facing his customers. It said:

> We no longer smoke in here.
> We've accomplished this with pride.
> So if you have to have a weed,
> then get your butt outside.

Chapter 8

"Disgusting," I muttered. But I bit my tongue, not wanting to change his resolve. I was thrilled he'd quit smoking. I just didn't like his poetry.

A week or so later I heard the dread words, "Fire! Fire!"

The beauty bark outside the front door was smoking—a customer had apparently come to buy insurance with a lit cigarette in his hand. Not finding an ashtray, he'd flipped it out the door.

The fire was minor. It didn't spread. But it opened Steve's eyes. The ashtrays reappeared, and one very obnoxious ditty disappeared.

Chapter 9

Turning thirteen is a big time in any kid's life. Steve and I decided to give that monumental event a special twist for our nephews Steve and John and niece, Wendi.

We'd enjoyed having their mother, Steve's sister Dodo, live with us for many a summer during her teen years. And those were the days when Steve sometimes worked two jobs, and I had to count every penny to let us enjoy the *good life*.

Now we could afford the largesse. The plan was to fly each one from Minneapolis to Sea-Tac, and then entertain them for a week or two. We always made sure that, on the *very day*, they were home in Coon Rapids to celebrate with their mom and friends.

In Minnesota the boys shared a small bedroom and fought like tomcats over their personal territory. (I'd observed this when I babysat while their mother was in the hospital.)

"It'll be good for Steve and John to get a taste of having their own space," I told Steve. "And for Wendi to be Queen Bee for a change."

Steve was first. We met him at the airport with hugs and proceeded to treat him like a king.

On the way home, we stopped at my favorite fruit stand and got a whole case of raspberries. I put them in the refrigerator and told nephew Steve, "Help yourself—whenever you want."

His eyes got big, and he said, "Really? As much as I want?"

"As much as you want," I verified.

"Gee, at home when we get raspberries—and that's almost never—Mom gets out four dishes. Then she puts one raspberry in each dish until

Chapter 9

the package is empty. That's about six berries for each of us. (Since her divorce, Dodo was a single mother trying to make it entirely on her own.) This is great!"

All of a sudden, looking worried, he asked. "Whenever I want?"

"Whenever," I assured him. "Only one rule."

I could almost hear him say to himself, "Yeah, always a rule to ruin things."

But when I finished my instructions, "Just quit before you get a stomach ache," he brightened up and asked, "Where are the spoons and dishes?"

Our nephew had his own suite upstairs—a cheery big room with a creek view and his own bath.

Probably the two biggest events we treated him to were going to a Seahawks football game in the King Dome and watching a first run of *Star Wars: Episode V—The Empire Strikes Back* at the Tacoma Mall Theater.

But just being alone with Steve was fun. I remember one day we walked up our hill and down Phillips Road for about a mile where we toured the fish hatchery and adjourning game farm.

It was a great visit.

John arrived a little more than two years later. Because he had a January birthday, we had to plan his trip during the Christmas holiday. Sadly, the Seahawks weren't scheduled for a home game during the days John was with us, but we tried to make everything special anyway.

I'd spent weeks baking and freezing my specialties in the freezer so I could offer our nephew enough Christmas goodies to fill his thirteen-year-old tummy. John was a good cookie eater.

He just plain liked to eat, so I included him in deciding what to have for dinner. I could hardly believe it one day when I was checking out a menu with John and he said, "Can we have cooked cabbage for our vegetable?"

Funny thing, after that my husband Steve decided he liked cabbage more than he had before. Now we have it often.

I had our entire house decorated for Christmas before John got there. But I'd saved buying the tree so the two of us could go out and have the fun of picking it out together.

Steve got it set up in the family room, and John and I decorated the tree with our mostly hand-made ornaments.

Out of the blue, John said. "At home I get to wrap all the presents."

It didn't take me long to latch onto *that*. John spent the rest of the day choosing paper, cutting, pasting, and bow-making. We'd never had such a beautiful array of creatively wrapped gifts.

Probably the highlight of that visit was when we saw *E.T. The Extra-Terrestrial*. Who can ever forget the touching love between Elliott and E.T.? And of course the quote of the decade: "E.T., phone home."

After John left, I told Steve, "Dodo's boys are keeping me young. I don't think I'd have gone to either *Star Wars* or *E.T.* if they hadn't gone with me."

Celebrating John's *early* birthday with him was probably the highlight of that Christmas season for Steve and me.

Wendi had a July birthday. *What in the world can I do with Wendi while I'm working?* The easy answer—I asked her to be my assistant.

The two of us had a lot of girl-talk-time as we drove back and forth to work. I taught her some essentials about filing and found her to be a quick study. At noon we walked half a block to a cute little neighborhood restaurant and had lunch.

But the frosting on Wendi's birthday cake turned out to be the paycheck I gave her on her last day of work. Her big smile said it all.

The Saturday before she had to return home, the Seahawks played in Seattle. We made a day of it. Steve and Wendi suffered through a few minutes (Steve said it was hours) at a great fabric store I loved while I picked out fabric for a new suit. Nordstrom's was more to Steve and Wendi's liking. They cruised the first floor while I checked out the shoe department.

When we put Wendi on the plane to go back to Minneapolis, I couldn't help but feel sad. This was the end of our *Thirteenth Birthday Bashes* with Dodo's three kids.

As Bob Hope said, "Thanks for the memories!"

My cup had indeed overflowed.

Chapter 10

OUR LIFE TOOK A detour one Saturday morning when our daughter Michele surprised us by showing up unexpectedly, sat on our family room sofa, and told us two things. One—her husband of almost nine years had moved out—permanently. Two—she was six weeks pregnant.

Steve and I looked at each other—immediately read our mate's mind (a seldom repeated miracle)—and promised, "We'll do whatever it takes to help you when the baby is born."

Thus, at age 51, I was on the verge of becoming a five-day-a-week, full-time nanny.

"How can you give up your career?" my shocked friends asked.

(These were the women who expressed their disgust when I'd confessed that Steve and I had a joint bank account. "Don't you realize his money belongs to both of you, and your money is yours?" they'd asked in amazement. They were the ones who rolled their eyes when I explained, "We have a partnership—we trust each other.")

No big deal, I thought. While I worked full time at our family business—and got paid for doing so—the insurance business was Steve's baby. Not mine. Insurance meant selling and working with numbers—two of my most hated endeavors. I looked forward to a respite.

Sure I'd had jobs before Steve and I started our insurance agency, but none of them were what I'd consider a career.

During my ten years as a stay-at-home mom, raising my two daughters, I'd been *driven* to do everything *perfectly*. That didn't give me much time to just *enjoy* my daughters.

I didn't wear pearls and high heels while doing my house work, but I guess, otherwise, I *was* June Cleaver. (My Michele recently told me she had a Beaver Cleaver childhood!)

Now, with the luxury of time, I had another chance at child rearing. *Hmm . . .*

My nanny days started when Sean was born. We were scheduled to babysit big brother, four-year-old Larry until Michele and the baby came home—maybe a day or two. Then she would have a month of maternity leave before she went back to work.

Instead, we had Larry for ten days—thanks to a real ugly case of the chicken pox. I noticed the first raised red bump when I gave my grandson his evening bath. *Mosquito bite?* Couldn't imagine *that* in late October. By morning the rash covered his tummy.

Having nursed my two girls through the pain and agony of this dread kid disease, I *knew*. I called the doctor for an oral medicine and directed Steve to pick up the prescription and some oatmeal soap. I knew I'd be giving lots of oatmeal baths.

Poor little Larry! It was bad enough he itched everywhere on his body at the same time, but not seeing his mother for ten days (doctor's orders because of the new baby) was tough. He lived for her phone calls. Thank goodness we already had a *Larry Room* at our house with his own bed and toys. At least he felt at home.

I read to him, played games, did projects. I remember turning a shoe-box into a *Bambi House* using color crayons, pieces of colored paper, and scrap fabric. He transformed some twigs we scavenged out in the woods into a darling Bambi. The fawn even had white (thanks to my shoe polish) spots.

The two of us made oatmeal cookies—I taught him how to break eggs—and he got to lick the beaters.

But I failed completely in one endeavor—art. "Draw a horse, Nanny," he said. I did my best.

"I hate to tell you," my grandson advised me in a serious voice, "but that's not a very good horse. Let me do it." Only days short of being four, Larry's drew a horse that looked so real it almost neighed.

Chapter 10

For two years after that (I'd signed up for a two-year stint of full-time daycare), I met my daughter and grandbaby at our family room door at 7:15 a.m. And—at 5:30 p.m.—delivered him back into her arms.

I was alone with Sean ten hours a day. Blessedly, happily, joyfully alone with Sean.

Sometimes I almost wanted time to stop so I could be a forever-nanny to my always-young grandsons.

First thing in the morning, I gave Sean his bottle. Played with him a while, then put him down for morning nap.

Then I did something—every day—that I'd never done in my whole life. While the baby was napping, I took time for myself.

I began collecting—motivational articles by Erma Bombeck and Norman Vincent Peale—quotations from John Ruskin and Alexander Solzhenitsyn, articles from *Guideposts* and quotes from the Bible. I put them in an *Affirmation Notebook* that I read daily. (Still using—am on my fourth edition—bigger every time.)

While I learned how to relax and meditate, I began my trip into becoming a different person.

When Sean woke up, we ate lunch—always a challenge. He didn't like beets.

Afterwards, I bundled him up (amount of clothes depending on the weather), took the stroller from the garage, adjusted his wiggly body in the canvas seat, and walked down the narrow road that winds up the hill and through virgin timber on its way to civilization—about a half mile.

Every day was an adventure. One day we saw a bunny. He added *bun* to his lexicon.

When we got back, I put Sean down for his afternoon nap. He slept until Steve got home.

Being a nanny was fun. I enjoyed my grandsons!

Some days Sean and I would *read* books. He'd tap his little feet with the rhythm of the rhyme. He loved looking at the pictures—making the animal sounds.

Ba Ba said the lamb. *Moo* said the cow.

Sometimes he'd swing in his swing or jump in his little jumper chair.

One afternoon, when I was taking him out of the jumper to put him down for his afternoon nap, he gave a little extra jump.

In the blink of an eye, I was immobilized. A loose curlicue wire drove itself under my wedding ring, ripping it apart. Almost as fast, the gold band of my ring sprang back, piercing the flesh of my finger. By one-eighth inch of skin, I was captive of a hooligan jumper chair that also held my now-crying grandson.

My God, I thought. *What should I do? Steve won't be home for three and a half hours.*

I tested the swing. It slid on the wood floor. Slowly, Sean and I—conjoined like fraternal twins—moved to the kitchen. I got the sharpest knife I had—pressed it to my finger—sawed until I hit metal—pulled. I was free—my finger bleeding. I grabbed the paper towel roll off its pedestal—pressed hard. Leaving Sean for a moment in the relative safety of his jumper chair, I ran to the bathroom, found a big Band-Aid, and put it on—as tight as I could.

Finally, I breathed. After freeing Sean, I rocked him until he calmed down.

When Steve got home, Sean was sleeping in his crib.

"You'll never believe . . . " I began. And I told my husband my story.

Steve changed his life also. While he'd worked nine-hour days forever—

7 a.m. to 5 p.m.—he decided to begin leaving at 4:00 so he could pick Larry up from day care. That gave him some extra time with his grandsons.

Initially Steve gave Larry some tracing paper from his own desk and the *World Book* volume on animals. Our oldest grandson began tracing—soon was drawing freehand. He turned out to be a budding artist. Five days a week he spent his late afternoons drawing animals. A family room end table became his drawing board. He filled the drawer beneath with dozens of pictures.

For minimal dollars, we kept our oldest grandson happy and busy for two years.

Larry's first horse drawing turned into a life-time love of art. (Last summer he had an oil painting—*Notre Dame by the Seine*—displayed in the Seattle Art Museum.)

One March day, my husband and Larry arrived just as Sean woke up. After setting up my artist-in-residence with a glass of milk and a cookie on the coffee table and his art supplies next to him, my husband and I took Sean outside to the swing set.

Life was good living on the banks of Chambers Creek. In summer the stream meandered from Steilacoom Lake a few miles away, past our place,

Chapter 10

and down to Puget Sound. When fall arrived so did the salmon that spawned in its waters. We loved watching them. Sometimes they stopped right in front of our windows, wiggling their posteriors into the gravel on the bottom of the creek as they laid their eggs.

On this particular spring day, the birds were singing. A crescendo of sound rose from the water—like crashing cymbals in an orchestra. I watched a single leaf. Saw it disappear in a millisecond as the creek lapped at the upper reaches of the rock wall we'd built to save our backyard during the annual spring rush of high water. Sometimes the depth exceeded five feet.

Steve pushed the kiddy swing. Sean's shrieks of joy remind me of our daughters when we first took them to Disneyland at ages seven and ten.

Then, saturated in motion, my husband stopped the swing, and lifted our precious grandson down. We walked toward the house leisurely, Sean by our side.

I wore a new pair of red shoes from Nordstrom's. I loved shoes.

One minute I was enjoying life, reveling in the glory of the setting. The next, I heard a splash.

Before I looked, I *knew*.

"Sean's in the water!" I shouted as I jumped into the raging creek.

I couldn't swim. I'm barely over five-feet tall. Yet I never worried for a second.

Floundering, I discovered a miracle—I could see!

I sensed him even before I saw Sean's curly head break the water. I reached out. Touched the nap of his corduroy overalls. Grabbed them as if my life—not just his—depended upon my speed and strength. In that instant, he *was* my life.

Sean's arms hugged my neck. I held him tight. Turned. Took a few tentative steps in the swift stream. Almost stumbled. Finally I saw Steve's fingers and handed him my precious bundle.

Sean was safe.

I'd never before experienced fearlessness. Or *total* love.

That day... For one precious moment... I'd been given the gift of both.

Both Steve and I remember those two years—the good and the bad—with much fondness.

Chapter 11

ONE OF THE PERKS of owning an insurance agency was qualifying for company trips. We made two—three-weeks each—that I will never forget.

Croatia—Three Weeks

Both sets of Steve's grandparents were from the part of Yugoslavia now called Croatia. In 1980 we decided to expand our company-paid-for week in Dubrovnik by fourteen days.

"Let's spend our extra time chasing your roots," I suggested.

Miracle of miracles, we found Steve's relatives—in a large part thanks to Ruza Arhanic, a professor at Zagreb University and a translator who'd been recommended to Steve before we left home.

We met Ruza the day we arrived in Zagreb. After a series of phone calls, she'd connected us to Stjepan Metulji. When Steve and Stjepan discovered they both had a grandmother named Ana Kruzich, Ruza said, "I'll make you a plan."

The next day we all met in Karlovac, about 90 kilometers south of Zagreb. Our plan—to find out how we were related.

It was a busy day.

(Details of this twenty-four hours are featured in a 38 chapter chronicle of our entire trip called *Darlene's Diary*.)

That evening, five of us (Ruza, Stjepan, Stjepan's father, Steve and me) sat in the home of a country priest looking through the pages of an old church record book he'd found in the rectory attic. The crumbling paper was so fragile that, as he turned pages, he held each single piece—one hand on top and the other on the back.

When we found the names of Steve's grandparents—Ana Kruzich and John (Ivan) Metulji, everyone cheered. Even the priest was excited. He

Chapter 11

brought out glasses and a bottle of Croatian sljivovica to toast our find with a jubilant, *Živjeli*.

Finding Steve's roots was a life-changing experience for me. That morning we'd all gathered in the nineteenth-century farmhouse where Stjepan's father and Steve's grandfather—had both been born. While sitting there, drinking sljivovica and eating bread fresh from the corner brick oven, a 17-year-old girl named Ljubica invaded my mind. I thought, *What if?* And I began my first novel, *Under the Gallus Frame*.

Second Three Week Trip—Croatia, Belgium, Denmark

Croatia—Again

We boarded a plane for Copenhagen in late April 1982. Then, on our dime, we took a Yugoslavian Air Line flight to Zagreb for a week with Steve's relatives in Croatia. This time we had English/Croatian and Croatian/English dictionaries. Plus Stjepan and his wife had taken English classes.

One of the highlights occurred when they took us to the birthplace of Steve's paternal grandmother. We still have the collage of photos Steve took that day. They hang on our dining room wall—between the original oil we bought from Anton Bahanek (a noted Croatian artist, famous for his work in the local style called "Nave") and an oil I painted of the Mostar Bridge.

Belgium

The second week we spent in Belgium, thanks to a big slice of synchronicity.

The previous June we'd unexpectedly connected with old Lakewood friends, Donna and Jim Tweedie, who were in the states on vacation. Jim, who worked for the lumber-giant Weyerhaeuser, was then located in Brussels.

"Come stay with us when you get to Europe," they'd said. "We've got a five-bedroom apartment and love company."

Fat chance, I thought. But I did save the business card Jim gave me.

Eight months later, Steve qualified for a trip to Denmark and a free week in Copenhagen.

When we called our friends, we found that Jim had just been told he was being rotated back to the U.S.—to Little Rock, Arkansas.

"We're going to take a week off to see all our favorite places starting the first of May. Come be our guests—I've got a company car."

We ended up having a private tour of Belgium while staying in luxury accommodations. Some of our favorite sites were Bruges, Ghent, and—at Waterloo—a museum that depicted the battle in miniature.

But perhaps the highlight was a trip to Antwerp where Jim brought us to the waterfront and onto a Weyerhaeuser ship. The longer-than-a-football-field vessel transported wood products world-wide.

Jim pointed and said, "See that? That's where we'll start. It's called the wheelhouse—it's the brains of the operation."

I looked—it was at least six stories up. When I took step three on the gangplank, I thought, *I can't do this*! (I have a terrible case of acrophobia—in third grade I almost fainted when the postmaster took us on the roof of the two-story Glasgow Post Office.)

Gritting my teeth, I kept telling myself—every single step. *You can do this, Darlene. You can do this.*

I'm *so* glad I did.

We were met by the captain as we exited the gangplank and taken up an elevator to his domain, the bridge. There, surrounded by windows that allowed us to view both sky and water, was the ship's steering wheel. He allowed me to touch it. It felt like I was putting my fingers on the knob of the door to the Gate of Heaven—scary, yet exciting.

Like he had all the time in the world, the captain explained his job. He showed us the maps he used to navigate through the channels from the dock onto larger and then larger, river-like bodies of water until they finally reached the North Sea. Each change of map—and there must have been hundreds although he only showed us a few—showed not only the channel itself, but the hidden sandbars that he needed to avoid. I love maps—I could have stayed there all day.

The captain invited us to lunch with him (a real honor Jim had arranged). I have no idea what I ate—I was too busy looking at the captain. Tall—probably 6 ft. 5 in.—he had the chiseled face of Rock Hudson and the ice-blue eyes of my well-loved Norwegian father.

Chapter 11

Copenhagen

Copenhagen was delightful. We took day trips, to Hamlet's Castle and across the North Sea by hydrofoil to Malmo, Sweden. I dined on reindeer (to the disgust of my animal-loving daughter, Michele).

Steve bought me a locket at Bing and Grondahl—pale-blue porcelain—featuring a perfect edelweiss—encased in heart-shaped gold. At Royal Copenhagen we chose a figurine of a little girl in a blue, one-piece swim suit. It reminded us of our two daughters—all decked up for swim team.

I spent so much time picking out nine perfect blue and white tiles (to be made into a special trivet when we got home), that Steve excused himself and went out outside to people-watch.

We saw six countries in three weeks.

Chapter 12

THERE MUST BE A rule somewhere that an empty space begs to be filled.

Michele was in college and Stephanie in high school in 1976 when we moved into our (technically) five bedroom, four bath home on Chambers Creek.

Some counseled, "Downsize."

We said, "Not us. We're just getting started."

Steve took over one room as his personal study—blithely allowing me to continually add books on the shelves of the floor-to-ceiling bookcase that covered a whole wall. (Steve had been a non-reader-for-pleasure when we married. It didn't take too long before he joined me in my reading vice.)

Another I filled with my sewing machine and the upright grand piano that no one played regularly. (It was kind of like my dear uncle Albert who lived with us for years—not adding all that much to our household but his presence, yet we never wanted to give him up.)

That left the master, Stephanie's bedroom, and a guest room.

Bobbie

Voila! Bobbie moved into our guest room for nine months.

One summer day in 1976 my childhood big-brother Bob Johnson (his parents and mine were best friends—he was seven years older) called looking for a home for his daughter while she attended Bellarmine Prep in Tacoma for her senior year of high school. They didn't live all that far away—Snoqualmie. But daily commuting wouldn't leave her any time for studying, extra-curricular activities, or just plain fun.

(Writing all these years later, I realize what a compliment Bob was giving Steve and me—trusting us with his much loved daughter. Retroactively, I say, *Thank you, Bob.*)

Chapter 12

Bobbie was a cheery, outgoing girl who fit in our family from day one. One of our first treats for our new expanded family was a dinner at The Spaghetti Factory. Yum!

Early on, our boarder arrived at the breakfast table dressed in bib overalls.

What's Steve going to do? I silently wondered. I knew he *hated* bib overalls.

(A few years before, our Michele had come down the stairs dressed in a pair she'd bought with her own money. Steve had blown a gasket. "You're not going out dressed like *that*!" he'd fussed. She'd argued a bit. Whined ... Went back to her room and changed ...)

I must say, he didn't say a thing to Bobbie for a full minute. Silence is *not* one of Steve's virtues. Finally, calmly he said, "I wouldn't let Michele and Stephanie wear those horrible *things* while they lived in my house. Since your dad asked us to treat you like one of our own daughters, I'm going to have to ask you to change."

Bobbie looked a bit chagrined. But she didn't argue. Instead, she turned around, went back to her room, and came down a while later in a pair of jeans.

That was the worst thing that ever happened during those nine months.

An unexpected plus to our new situation was that Bob and I got reacquainted. Growing up, our two families got together for every holiday and constantly in between.

During the frigid winter of 1951, his brother Gail had lived at our house the whole month of January and the first two weeks in February. (They lived four miles north of town—his dad had to bring him to town on a horse because the snow had drifted and blocked the roads.) We were like family.

Now the six of us—Bob, his wife Pat, Bobbie, Steve, Stephanie, and yours truly—made new memories.

It helped me *so* much when Bob and Pat attended my dear Daddy's funeral that February at St. John Bosco in Lakewood. They came down to our house afterwards. Spent time with my mother and us. The past and present melded.

That spring, Bobbie was in a school musical, *Little Miss Sunshine*. Steve and I had a pre-play dinner at our house for all of us before we went to see the play. We used our brand new microwave to cook prime rib. *Warning!*

Never Cook Prime Rib in a Microwave. Steve was devastated—he prided himself on making gourmet meals.

But the play was fun.

A little side note: later that summer when Bobbie came to visit, she was wearing bib overalls—and a big grin.

We all had a good laugh.

The Hideki and Mike Interlude

A couple of years later Stephanie bought her own condo and moved out. At that time we had two vacant bedrooms and a bath.

Then Hideki arrived.

Steve was chairman of the Rotary International Student Exchange program in 1980. We signed right up as hosts for the second three months. *Only three months.*

We should have realized what was in store in August when we got a letter from Hideki's Japanese father. It read: "Please know, you have my permission to beat my son whenever he is bad."

Then, when we picked Hideki up at Sea-Tac, we noticed that when we asked him a question he had to stop and write on his arm before he answered.

"Looks like his English needs some help," Steve said.

The first three months Hideki lived with a local chiropractor and his wife Sharon.

They didn't complain. But they did warn us, "He's a loner."

We planned activities for three months.

Hideki moved in with us the first of December. Our goal for the next three months was to make him feel like one of the family.

We made Christmas special. He was the guest of honor at our annual Christmas brunch. His under-the-tree gift was a black-felt cowboy hat. We took him everywhere.

In January we treated Hideki to an all-day trip to Seattle for a Seahawk game in the King Dome. He took lots of pictures. When Steve bought him his very own football helmet he actually grinned—first one we'd seen.

By February, we'd run out of big ideas.

Try as we might, we couldn't get him connected with either kids in school or adults in the community. He didn't want go to basketball games.

Chapter 12

He ignored our offers to bring some of his friends over. (We began to wonder. Had he made *any* friends?)

Toki, the head waitress at The Lakewood Terrace, our favorite restaurant, invited him to her house for a real Japanese meal. He declined. Other Rotarians asked him to dinner or sporting events.

"No, no," Hideki said. "Too busy. Too much school work."

Our son-in-law spent an afternoon with Hideki. Larry had been an exchange student himself in England, and he stressed the opportunity our boarder was missing.

I talked to Hideki. Discovered that his father expected him to keep up his classes in his regular school in Japan *besides* going to school in Lakewood. He got his assignments by mail—he returned them upon completion. (No wonder the kid had so much mail coming and going! And I'd thought he was popular back home.)

Steve fussed, "He's just plain boring!"

"Don't worry," I said. "In March he'll be moving to the next host family. Then we'll be down to one extra—Mike."

We'd been surprised in early January 1981 when Steve's sister had called and begged Steve to help her son. "Mike quit school in Chicago. He's back in Butte. Do something!" she'd ordered.

Knowing that, even with Hideki in Stephanie's old room, Michele's was still empty. And—since we'd just let an under-achieving employee go—we had an opening at the insurance agency—Steve said, "Send Mike over."

In early January, our family room got pretty full when we were all watching TV.

Of course, the only time Hideki showed up was when he heard the music that introduced the hit of the season, *Charlie's Angels*. He loved pretty American girls! Three on screen? Our number one boarder was in a permanent state of *Wow*.

I'd taught Hideki how to do some household chores. That included doing his laundry and changing his bed each week. But I cleaned all the bathrooms.

When I'd had been sprucing up the house for our annual Christmas brunch, I noticed the upstairs bathroom had a strange odor—even after I cleaned.

By the end of January the bathroom smell was much worse. Gingerly, I got down on my hands and knees and *really looked*. To my amazement, the white and yellow (with a splash of orange) plaid wallpaper behind and beside the toilet had turned into a three-dimensional yellow glob. Getting closer, I gagged.

Someone had not been hitting the toilet bowl. I knew in a flash that it had *not* been Mike.

I mentioned the problem to my nephew.

"I hadn't known what to tell you," he'd confessed. "Glad you were the one to bring it up. I think it's an *aiming* problem."

"I agree," I said. "But since I just had girls, I've no practice teaching a little boy how. And Hideki isn't little. Steve will blow a gasket. I don't want to ask him. Could you? Would you?"

Mike did. I never asked how. I just scraped off the smelly residue. The problem never came back.

In March, Steve couldn't find a third host family to take our exchange student. Not one of the over 100 Lakewood Rotary members volunteered. We ended up with Hideki for six months instead of three. The last three seemed to take forever. We'd done everything extra we could think of in our first quarter.

About the only excitement occurred one April morning.

Mike didn't come down to breakfast. I called upstairs, "Hey, Mike, your eggs are getting cold." No Mike.

I rushed outside. Mike's car wasn't on the driveway.

Mystified, I started back inside. It was breezy out. I saw a piece of folded paper being blown back and forth.

After I picked it up, I wished I could turn my life back a day. Fix whatever was the matter.

The note was short.

I've decided to move back to Butte. Bye.

Mike and I had watched TV together the night before. Then we'd played a couple of games of Scrabble before I went to bed at eleven. He hadn't said a word about leaving.

Steve and I were both crushed. We'd given him free board and room and an entry-level job. We'd paid him the same as his predecessor—*he'd*

Chapter 12

been in training. Being a family owned business, he could have advanced to the top.

He chose to disappear.

Why?

He never said.

In late May, Steve bemoaned the fact that he hadn't been able to offer our exchange student more side trips. Rising to the occasion, he called a fellow Rotarian in Canada and talked him into sponsoring Hideki for the remainder of the exchange year and showing him the sites in Vancouver and Victoria.

When it came time to pack, Hideki filled his suitcases and told me, "I've got a lot more. I need some boxes." I went to Fed Ex. Got four.

Since he was limited to two suitcases for his overseas flight, we agreed to mail the extra separately.

We drove Hideki to Canada, said goodbye, and returned to our empty home. That is, empty except for the boxes sitting in the middle of our hall.

The next day Steve came back from the airport in shock—with the boxes still in the trunk of our car.

"You can't believe how much money it'll cost to get Hideki's extras to Japan! Rotary won't pay that much, and I'm not about to fork up a fortune either. I swear, the kid must have been collecting rocks all the time he lived with us!"

Well—it wasn't rocks!

We opened the boxes and found mostly magazines. A total of 30. Every single issue of *Playboy, Penthouse,* and *Hustler* issued while Hideki lived in Lakewood.

On a hunch, Steve opened each one—only the June issues still had the Centerfolds.

"Must have packed the girly-pictures in his suitcase," Steve said. He laughed and added, "I'd love to be there when Hideki opens the box we *do* send and finds only his cowboy hat, Seahawk helmet and assorted mementoes."

We got everything into one big box. Put the magazines in the trash. Rotary paid the lesser/reasonable charge.

That was the end of that!

Or so we thought . . .

A couple of years later, on Steve's birthday, the kids were all at our house one Sunday to celebrate with their dad. Since he was born on April 1, they'd always had fun with him. (It seemed the jokes got better/worse as time went on.)

When we saw a figure go by both kitchen windows, Michele, Stephanie, and I got very busy.

The back doorbell rang.

"Can you get it, Dad?" Michele called.

The rest of us peeked as Steve opened the family room door. We heard a young man declare, "Western Union, sir. Please sign."

Looking perplexed, Steve opened the envelope. Read the telegram:

> Mr. Matule ... S T O P
> Am arriving at Sea-Tac ... S T O P
> 3:47 p.m. today ... S T O P
> Please pick me up ... S T O P
> Hideki ... S T O P

"I can't believe this!" Steve yelled as he threw the offending paper toward the ceiling.

And we all said, "April Fool."

Chapter 13

OUR INSURANCE BUSINESS (for Steve considered it to be a mutual endeavor even though his father would adamantly disagree that a woman should be awarded such a designation) was profitable. Life was good.

Steve was a commissioner for the Lakewood Fire District, active in Rotary and Chamber of Commerce (as president, he helped plan the development of a new shopping mall in Lakewood). I was president of Lakewood Women in Business.

Business at the agency was booming.

Over the years we'd bought and remodeled an old house on Gravelly Lake Drive for our insurance office.

We'd remodeled our home, adding a large TV room over the garage, and a Jacuzzi room adjacent to the master bath.

Around that time, I remember running into some Lakewood people one evening while having dinner at the top of the new Sheraton in downtown Tacoma. One woman, manager of a major bank, said, "Well . . . it must be nice to be able to just sit around and count your money." I was hurt—both Steve and I worked hard. We'd done well. But no one had helped us. We'd done it on our own. (Or so we thought.)

About then, we started making mistakes.

We joined two other businessmen in a partnership that built a 25,000 square foot office building on our vacant property. Opulent, with expensive rent, we hadn't been able to get any tenants other than Matule Insurance. We lost our financial stake.

We didn't give up—rented new office space.

It had been a bad day.

People move. Change offices. Homes. Sometimes even spouses.

As close as Steve and I were, we'd always looked at his insurance business in a much different way. For Steve it was not only his livelihood—his business was literally his life. He loved it. He *lived* it.

Me? I'd come in by the side door—the one labeled *Duty*.

I've chronicled my dislike of "owning your own business" before in this story. But the truth was, I didn't really know what I *did* want to do when I grew up.

I became a Home Economics major in college because I loved sewing. And decorating.

At age fifteen, I'd talked my parents into letting me upholster their living room sofa and matching chair. If I can give myself a pat in the back at this late date, I'll say this—I did a professional job. It was a challenge, and I loved it.

But in the nineteen fifties, about all I could do with my college degree was to teach Home Ec. I remembered the unmotivated, giggling seventh grade girls who'd barely finished their required apron, when I'd gone on to make three dresses.

My mother said, "Well, Darlene, you can come back to Glasgow and be the alteration lady at The Fashion Shoppe."

I wanted none of either!

So I got married. Sewed—*everything*—from Vogue-inspired dresses for my daughters to ball gowns for me. I crafted draw-drapes, upholstered, quilted. I gardened.

I'd been the interior designer of the office complex we'd just lost. That had been fun. But leaving all my hard work for someone else to enjoy? It had torn me to the core.

Only weeks after moving from our palatial two-story office building, Steve and I were sitting on our Creekside patio after dinner. Both of us were feeling raw.

I don't remember what was said—probably for the best—but I took offense. I dashed inside, grabbed my purse, and drove up our windy hill. Away from my upset husband.

With nowhere to go—I couldn't face anyone—I headed to our new, rented office.

I ran inside, made a right into the first little office, and dropped to the carpet. Sobbed until there were no tears left.

When I finally gathered myself together, I drove home.

Chapter 13

Steve's car was gone when I arrived.

I tore inside. Instinct carried me to our bedroom—our closet. His clothes were gone.

Where did he go? I anguished.

I knew he hadn't gone to our office. I drove by Lynn's house—she was the closest. No Steve. Michele's home was about a half-mile away. I sped there. No car.

Desperate, I drove to the Lakewood Terrace—where his friends often had dinner and gathered later for a drink or two. I went up and down the parking lot—twice in case I hadn't seen his car through my tears. No sign.

In agony, I turned my car homeward. It seemed like it took me hours to drive that five-minute ride.

Bring Steve home! I shouted silently. Over and over again.

The house was dark when I arrived. The driveway clear. The garage looked like an empty tomb when I opened it.

I prayed.

Frantic prayers. *Please, God, don't let him have an accident!*

Promissory prayers. *If You bring Steve home, I'll suck it all up. I'll never complain again.*

I dropped to my bed. Fell asleep praying, *Dear God . . .*

The ceiling lights awakened me.

Steve was home. Shattered, but home.

We slept in the same bed that night. Never touching. Never talking.

The next morning we did talk. Things were still tense.

"I was going away. Forever," he said.

"I'm sorry," I offered.

He shrugged.

I made bacon and eggs for him. He ate, silent, then left for work.

It took a while to heal. But we learned two big lessons:

> *Never leave when you're angry.*
> *Our love was bigger than our pride.*

Together, we made our rented office *ours*.

Then we bought a Seattle insurance agency from the widow of a friend who'd passed away suddenly—agreed to a five-year pay-off.

Steve and I had it all figured out. I'd concentrate on the Seattle office while Steve kept the Lakewood business running smoothly. In five years I'd be able to retire.

The two years I commuted to Seattle changed our lives in more than one way.

Driving up wasn't a problem—it just took an hour. Coming back home proved to be another thing entirely. I tried to leave around four to miss the bad traffic, but found there never was a good time.

Rainy nights were worst. (Please remember, it rains *a lot* on I-5 between Seattle and Tacoma.) Big semis zoomed past me like we were in a hydroplane race on Lake Washington, their rooster-tails almost drowning my car. Often it was six before I dragged in our back door.

Dear Steve took up the slack and had dinner ready to eat whenever I arrived. I thanked my lucky stars for having such a good husband.

However . . . Even with my new job up north, I still paid the American Express bills. One day I opened their monthly statement to find that we owed over $500 to a publishing company. *Must be a mistake.*

One phone call revealed that twenty-three volumes of the *Grand Diplome Cooking Course* had indeed been mailed to our address.

I came unglued. *How could he? Didn't he realize we were having a hard time paying for our new satellite office?*

"What in the world were you thinking?" I demanded of the culprit—Steve.

The ensuing conversation is censored.

I must admit though—from that day on, Steve *truly* became a gourmet cook. The books worked—he never made another *Purple Stew.*

I began my seventy-five mile trek (round trip) north four days a week.

It'll be worth it, I told myself as I drove on I-5 twice every day. *Remember, in five years, after we make the final payment, I can retire. Finally I'll be able to do something just for me.*

That dream proved to be financially impossible.

The agent we hired for the satellite decided to pay his overdue house payments by writing a company check. *How he could have been so dumb?* Being $4,500 short in our bank account didn't escape me very long.

Chapter 13

Minus an agent, it was all on me. True I was *licensed*. I'd taken the classes—passed the tests. But I'd never once gone out on a cold call. And didn't want to begin. It proved to be impossible to grow the business without someone prospecting clients outside the office.

The widow declined to renegotiate. Held us to the stiff monthly payments. We sold the Seattle satellite—paying her off in full. But at a price—we didn't make a dollar on our two year investment.

My energy sagged.

I kept thinking. *We had it all. Where did it go? Why?*

Back in Lakewood, I started stopping to pray at St. Francis Cabrini again.

Steve also had his share of business problems.

A disgruntled agent he'd let go for a poor attitude sued us. Our lawyer said, "It's a nuisance suit. I'll take care of it. Don't worry." We believed him.

A week before the trial, the attorney dumped us.

The judge said, "I'm not changing the date. It's your problem."

Our new attorney tried, but he was young and only had a week to get a case assembled.

It was a disaster. Instead of getting money back (which lawyer #1 had promised), we ended up paying $42,000 dollars!

The next week one of our largest companies (where we had almost a third of our policies placed) informed us they were not going to be representing our insurance agency anymore.

What would be next? I worried.

Steve's blood pressure skyrocketed.

We needed to do something. But what?

Chapter 14

"How'd you like to retire into a motel?" Steve asked one evening in late July.

I ignored him. We'd long joked about Steve's Aunt Ellie's statement that she was going to quit working and retire into a motel. I was not in the mood for joking.

My folks had owned a small motel. Running it had been far from a retirement. I might be ready to stop working at our insurance agency, but a motel was ludicrous. That was hard work! In eastern Montana you had to earn a year's income in four and a half months. It was a vicious circle—slave then worry. I wanted none of that!

"Listen," Steve said. "I've got a plan. There's a Tacoma agency that's interested in buying us out. And, I've got a lead on something that looks perfect."

"Perfect" was a travel agency franchise.

We'd gotten a taste of world traveling from the two trips our main insurance company financed. We wanted to do more.

Steve was right about starting the insurance agency, I thought. *Maybe I worry too much.*

༄

The deal went together—*Fast.*

Without taking time... Time to pray about what we *should* do...

With egotistic pride guiding us... *We've run a successful business for years*...

With some due-diligence—but not enough...

With attorney help—but not enough...

With blinders on...

We paid our franchise fee—*Huge*—half as much as it cost to have our creek house built.

In August, immediately after we signed our contract, the Franchise Guru brought us both up for a week in Vancouver, British Columbia—combination travel school and fun. "One of our *freebies*. Enjoy!" they said. Then they swooped Steve down to Miami for a Princess Ship tour (another freebie).

Steve was excited, "I'll be able to really *sell* again. I've missed that."

We both had visions of European tours and basking on tropical beaches.

"You'll own a first class travel agency," the Franchise Guru told us. We basked in our good fortune.

Overhead was significant from the start. The *to-do* list was long and specific. After leasing a large office on the busiest street in Lakewood, we remodeled the building and furnished two private suites plus the main office. We hired two travel professionals (no small monthly cost) and bought light-wool teal uniforms for everyone—Steve and me, both employees. Finally, we invited a hundred of our nearest and dearest personal and business friends to a lavish open house, complete with expensive plane tickets as door prizes.

On September 30, we got the bill for our first monthly franchise fee. What a shock! We'd understood it was a percentage of the gross. Thus it would be one amount if we took in $100 and a much different one if we'd made $100,000. We'd barely had the doors open that September.

When confronted, the Franchise Guru said, "You misunderstood. But don't worry. You'll be grossing over a hundred grand a week before you know it."

We were assured.

Next lesson—the airlines took their 90 percent directly from our bank account every Monday on any flights we'd booked the previous week. No wiggle room there.

"Ten percent commission doesn't go very far," I complained.

"We'll have to make it up on volume," Steve said.

Just before the snow flew, the Franchise Guru sent us to Sun Valley to play at the elegant Elk Horn Resort for a few days. Another *freebie*.

We began taking money from our personal account to pay our business bills.

In February we took a Franchiser jaunt to the Big Island. (That trip proved to be our last *freebie*.)

Steve kept adding clients. There never seemed to be enough.

The Franchise Guru said we had to hire another specialist to take care of the increase in customers.

We declined. That did not go well.

In August we invited the Franchise Guru to our creek home for a one-on-one meeting. We planned to cut our losses and get out of the travel business.

"You can't quit now," he said, "You're on the cusp of greatness."

Looking back, our location choice for the meeting was probably a terrible idea.

After leaving the main road, the long driveway to our home went through the lot-sized side garden we'd developed over the years. From our front door all you could see was our west garden. And trees—a forest seemingly reaching for heaven.

From our comfy lawn chairs on the patio where we sat, we looked directly on the shimmering water of Chambers Creek. The neighbors' lovely homes across the creek resembled Monet paintings.

As our friend Lynn had said many years before, it looked like we lived on an estate.

Thinking he had two wealthy patsies, The Franchise Guru prodded, played the *quitter* card, reminded us of the fortune we were almost abandoning.

We caved. Perhaps the worst decision of our entire lives.

What was supposed to be face-saving turned into financial suicide.

Steve worked like a man possessed. I dug further and further into our reserves to fund our personal life and pay the monthly shortages in the travel agency.

Once, when we were in Minnesota visiting family, Steve had to make a long-distance phone call to our banker one Monday morning to borrow enough money to pay the airline automatic withdrawal for the previous week's business.

Chapter 14

The end of August we shut the doors.
In two years we lost enough money to fund our retirement.

༄

Our bad luck continued.
Next, we found that our legal counsel on our insurance agency sale had been flawed. The buyer of our agency demanded we renegotiate monthly payments to a lesser amount. Much less.
Our new attorney said, "Your mistake—you have to do it."
We were way past *it comes in threes*. What was happening?

༄

Suddenly, Steve needed a job. Although his insurance license was still in force, he couldn't begin another independent insurance business of his own. He had a non-compete agreement with the buyer/new owner of Matule Insurance.
Discouraged, he finally took a job as a *new* agent for one of the *captive* big companies. That was about nine and a half steps down the ladder of success.

༄

And so it happened that in September 1989 I was looking for a job to pay our house payment.
I contacted three job agencies. Dressed in my best navy blue business suit, pearls, and high heels.
"You're not hirable," the first agency told me. "You don't have any references. All you did for the last thirteen years was work in a family business—that doesn't count."
At the second agency, they said, "The best we can do is a job in a big supermarket giving out samples—for minimum wage."
The third woman smiled and said, "I'd be happy to help. Just give me $3,000—cash—and I'll get you a job." I told her where to go.
Discouraged—*I'd been the business manager of our insurance agency. I'd hired and fired. I'd been a working partner*—I registered with a temporary employment group. For a couple of weeks, I'd worked off and on. One Thursday—jobless—I was home. Worrying. The phone rang at 4:39. "Got a one-day job for you," the chirpy voice of the temp lady said.

I came *so* close to laughing at her. But when she said it was for a special project at Hillhaven, I reconsidered. Hillhaven was a highly respected nursing home chain whose main office was in downtown Tacoma. I'd just sent them an application. *It'll be a good way to check them out*, I told myself.

That split second decision—to work for $5.00 an hour—for one day—turned into fifteen and a half years of upwardly mobile employment.

For the first four months I worked on a special *change-of-ownership* (CHOW) project—in a windowless room deep in the bowels of what at one time had been the local Sears store (where Steve had managed his crew of Allstate insurance agents when we first moved to Tacoma).

That first Friday, the boss, Kelley (who I judged to be about the same age as my daughters), asked me to come back the following Monday.

On Monday she asked, "Do you feel comfortable making calls? Randy (the other person working on the project) hates to talk to strangers on the phone."

"No problem," I said. "I've been doing phone work for thirteen years." *So much for that employment agency lady who said I didn't have any experience!*

Four months later—when the CHOW was finished—they hired me in the Reimbursement Department as a secretary. The next January I was promoted to the Licensure and Certification Department (where Kelley worked as Director). In the next fourteen years I did many a CHOW.

But—for the first time ever—I felt poor. My young *director* dressed like a fashion plate, took month-long vacations at a Maine resort, and was remodeling a Victorian house in a posh Seattle area.

Then I met a new hire in another department who was a step above me in the pecking order. To my amazement, I saw she only had one outfit—a black pant suit with a white shirt. (She must have rinsed out her blouse every night—it always looked crisp.) I discovered she was a recent divorcee who had three kids—a single mother who'd been forced to return to the work place.

I felt humbled. I thought of the twenty-plus suits in my walk-in closet. *I'm rich and don't even know it!* I thought guiltily.

Hillhaven was a great place to work. I made many friends (Kelley among them).

Chapter 14

Then the company had a scare—a hostile take-over attempt. Management weathered that storm, but the company was put into play. They got an *offer-they-couldn't-refuse*. The company sold to a Kentucky hospital chain that decided to move the whole Hillhaven operation to Louisville.

The new company courted me. Paid for Steve to fly to Louisville in January to see how he liked the area. He loved it.

In March they gave me a week off from my Tacoma job and flew Steve and me to Louisville. Put us up in one of the best hotels. Said, "We're a first-class business—you have an unlimited expense account."

We loved the area—the architecture, the rolling green hills, the *fun* things happening daily. We'd arrived the week of the Final Four basketball tournament for the national championship. Kentucky won! The celebration in our hotel lobby was something to experience!

The house prices were fantastic—we could get a home for much less than in Tacoma. We talked it over.

Sell our Creek place at Tacoma prices. (The company promised to pay the real-estate fee—so no cost to us.)

Buy at Louisville prices.

What wasn't to like?

A place called Polo Fields appealed to us. With a small down payment we commissioned a new home, right on the golf course. We chose everything, floor plan, color of each room, cabinets—down to the hardware. Even the outside brick.

They wanted me right away. My new job was to set up the whole licensure and certification department—my way.

Our house hadn't sold. "No problem. We'll put you up in an apartment immediately. If your place hasn't sold by the time the new house is done, we'll buy it ourselves."

I didn't leave my Chambers Creek dream home easily.

We *were* moving into a brand new house—you'd have thought I'd be happy. But the Kentucky place being 1,200 square feet smaller, I had to get rid of lots of stuff. And I must admit, I loved my stuff.

We didn't have a lot of time. After two garage sales . . . After giving the doll house Steve and I had been building to an inner city kindergarten . . . There was still one major thing left—the Christmas castle Steve and I had so lovingly built and decorated.

"It's got to go," Steve said. "I guess I'll have to call Goodwill."

"Goodwill is not an option!" I cried. "I don't want *just anyone* having it."

Our final, mutual choice of disbursal was drastic—we decided to cremate it.

Just before Steve lit the match that April day, I'd snatched the baby grand piano and all the castle furniture. Holding a plastic grocery sack filled with miniatures, I watched as flames licked through twenty years of memories.

That last day I remember sobbing as I knelt on my knees—scrubbing the kitchen floor. My tears fell on the vinyl and melded with the wash water.

After the movers left and I'd cleaned my way through all 3,600 square feet of house, it was time to leave.

I spent my few final minutes at the edge of Chambers Creek praying. *Please God, help me.* Steve and I had made what we thought was our best choice for our future life.

But had we?

Chapter 15

WE ARRIVED IN LOUISVILLE on April 26, 1996.

It was Derby Time. The CEO was on the board of Churchill Downs. He took the entire office to Dawn at the Downs—an opportunity to stand right at the edge of the track at 7 a.m. and watch the jockeys exercise their horses. Then eat a sumptuous brunch.

What a way to begin!

On Mother's Day, I was given box seats at The Downs for Steve and me. I'd always loved horse racing—had spent many a day with my friend Phyllis at the Valley County Fair sharing the $2 to bet on each race. (We made money!)

When Steve's sister and her husband Ray surprised me on my sixtieth birthday (they'd flown in from St. Paul—come straight to my office), I was able to get a box for the four of us that weekend.

I won $20.

Everything was great. Our house was ready to occupy. We'd move on the first of June. The company was buying our Tacoma house.

Then, on May 26, I stayed up later than Steve—writing *Thank You* letters to Tacoma friends who'd given us a beautiful going-away party. When I finished, I discovered a stack of letters. One from the company. *How could I have missed that earlier?*

Quickly I opened it. The bottom fell out of my world.

The letter explained that one of the three appraisals had been $100,000 lower than the other two. That changed the company's buyout contract—allowed them to take the lowest bid. And—because of the nullification of the contract—they weren't even obligated to pay the real estate fee.

How could that be?

Before we'd agreed to go with the company's offer, being cautious, we'd personally paid for an appraisal. The appraiser quoted a substantial selling price. "Might vary $5,000. No more." That didn't surprise us—we had a beautiful, recently updated, on-the-water home. After selling our place at Tacoma prices, we were going to have a minimal mortgage on our new house. After, when the dust settled, we'd have no other debt. We had everything well planned.

The check enclosed almost burned my fingers. It was for just under $5,000! Totally!!!

I cried all night long. Never slept a wink. Called in sick the next morning.

I made an appointment with the vice president who had been my mentor during the moving process. Showed him my copy of the appraisal we'd paid for prior to deciding to take the company deal. Explained we'd have never moved had we known we wouldn't get a fair price for our house.

"This is worse than not making me the head of the Licensure and Certification Department like I was promised," I said. (When I got to Louisville, I found they'd hired a man who'd never even worked in that section of health care as manager.) "I bit that bullet because you promised you'd take good care of me."

He assured me, "There's nothing the company can do." He didn't say the words, but the message was clear—"It's a done deal."

We lost our dream house. Couldn't close. The builder let us rent a smaller one in another area he was developing. "We'll keep the initial down payment until you have the total needed."

We were expecting a check from Steve's last Tacoma employer—decided we could close on the little house later. (Not what we expected—but the best we could do, considering the circumstances.)

The check came. We could have barely made the minimum down payment. But with only my income (Steve's promised job had also fallen through after we'd moved—the good-old-boy Southern network was working and excluded him at the last minute) we couldn't get a loan.

We were 2,000 miles away from home. In six weeks, we'd gone from being on the top of the world to floating in space.

Stephanie and Jake lightened our spirits when they visited. Jake loved two things that July—cranberry-raspberry juice and animals. Since you can't feed a toddler twenty-four hours a day, we spent a lot of time in zoos.

Chapter 15

At the first—the Louisville Zoo—he wanted to keep going back to the lion exhibit. "Fierce," he kept saying. I have no idea how old that King of the Beasts was, but I'm sure it had been years since he'd been anywhere near fierce. I doubt he had a single tooth in this mouth.

The second, Henry's Ark, was off the beaten path—about ten miles from Louisville—just outside the rural town of Prospect. My hairdresser who had a six-year-old recommended it. "Bring a loaf of bread and a lots of carrots," she'd said.

It was the epitome of a petting zoo. With a minimum of fences, many of the animals walk up and round winding paths looking for handouts. (I'm sure they're adequately fed, but free is free.)

There were dozens of photo opportunities—Stephanie must have used two or three rolls of film. She took a great picture of Jake cuddled up by a brown and white baby calf—his arm around its neck.

Chickens of many breeds, hens and roosters, wandered at will. There were also goats, deer, pigs, bunnies, peacocks, emus, ostriches, water buffalo, and a single zebra.

And camels . . . In the distance they were cute. But my perception changed quickly when one decided I was lunch. At least that's what I felt like as the camel looked at me with its beady eyes and charged.

A full camel-head taller than my over-six-foot husband, it towered over me. It's nostrils were flared, teeth bared. I felt like raw hamburger about to be consumed.

"Steve!" I yelled. "Help!"

But did Steve, or Stephanie, or even little Jake start waving their arms to change the dromedary's direction? Did one of them run for the owner, a worker?

No!

Then, as the brown beast lurched for my hand, I gave one more, terrified "Help!"

And they giggled. They chortled. They bent over laughing.

Abandoned by my family, I was desperate. I threw the whole bag of carrots at the animal whose teeth were about to tear into my arm.

And what happened? Did Steve run between me and my attacker? Did Stephanie shout for help? Did Jake cry, "Someone, please help my nanny!"

Absolutely not. They continued laughing as they watched the camel shake the bag of carrots open and help himself to lots of camel candy.

I must say, it took me a long time to collect myself from my near death experience. My family still thinks it's hilarious.

Me? I learned how to thwart these evil animals. Carrots will be my weapon.

Chapter 16

THAT YEAR WE PREPARED for our first ever Christmas without family. There was no way we could afford two round-trip plane tickets to Tacoma. It was a bittersweet experience.

But we had each other—and our dear miniature Schnauzer, Shadow.

We managed to buy presents for our daughters and grandsons—none for each other. But we splurged for the fixings of a special holiday dinner—Christmas Day was on Wednesday that year.

When I got home from work Monday night, Steve was beside himself.

"Shadow's disappeared!" he cried.

"My God! What happened?" I asked.

"I wish I knew," he choked. "After I got home, I took her for a walk—like always. Down the street behind us . . . Where they're building all those new houses . . .

"I started dinner. Turned on the TV—was listening to the news. I didn't think twice about letting her out back when she stood at the sliding glass door and whined—like she does when she has to go.

"Five minutes later, I went to let her in. No Shadow. Our backyard was empty.

"I rushed outside. Called and called. Nothing. Took off down the street. Retraced every step Shadow and I'd made before."

"She never wanders," I said. "What could have happened?"

"Believe me," he said, "I've been doing nothing but thinking for two hours. And I hate to tell you—but I'm afraid she was snatched!"

"Snatched?"

"Stolen! Grabbed! I should have known that guy was up to no good."

"What guy?" I asked.

"One of the workers at the new house behind us. He grilled me about Shadow. 'Your dog a real Schnauzer?' he asked. 'She got papers?'"

My stomach felt like a five-pound brick had raced through my esophagus, hit bottom, and bounced twice before landing.

Steve and I scoured the neighborhood 'til dark, until we couldn't see further than a foot in front of us.

Shadow was nowhere.

We both broke down when we got home.

That night I put her bed out on the front porch—left a bowl of food beside it—just in case.

It was cold that night... Twenty degrees on our outside thermometer. *Could she possibly survive?*

The next day—Christmas Eve—I had to work until noon. Steve spent the morning checking the local pounds. Nothing.

Five years before, Stephanie, Michele, and I had joined to buy Steve a special Christmas gift—a three-month-old miniature German Schnauzer. From the beginning, wherever Steve went, his dog followed—hence her name—Shadow.

Now—when we'd already lost so much that year—Shadow disappeared from our lives.

It's not fair! I yelled silently so I wouldn't make it harder on my husband.

Up until then, Shadow had been Steve's dog. Exclusively.

I just *liked* her—or so I thought. Now that she was gone, I realized I'd grown to love her.

Every evening after Shadow's disappearance, I warmed her bed and—just as I was ready to go upstairs to sleep—put it on the front porch with a dish of fresh dog food.

Nothing. Night after night.

Steve cooked French toast the next Sunday morning. We missed the click of Shadow's toenails when she rushed to the kitchen—on point when she smelled the batter. Steve always cooked extra, knowing how much she loved it. Now we remembered how Shadow sat at our feet those days as she ate out of her dish. To tell you the truth, it was hard to swallow that first Sunday.

Every night I sat in my favorite chair and automatically patted my left knee. But no little ball of black fur jumped into my lap. I missed the twelve-pound *blanket* I'd come to cherish.

Chapter 16

Steve kept checking with the pound. He read the *Lost and Found* in the *Courier-Journal*. It was as if Shadow had disappeared into thin air.

The champagne I ceremoniously drank every New Year's Eve tasted flat that year. After nine days of *nothing*, I sadly gave up.

On New Year's Day, Steve opened up the paper and whooped.

"Look at this!" he cried. "Found! Black German Schnauzer!"

But his joy was short lived. He called the number. Was told, "We had that darling little dog for seven days. But she disappeared last night when the neighbors were shooting off their holiday fireworks."

Still, we got their address—about a half mile away—on the other side of the vacant property next to us.

"She's somewhere out there," I said. "We'll find her."

Steve and I put on our boots and trooped on foot across no-man's land.

"Maybe she'll smell our scent," he said.

I prayed.

We stopped and talked to the couple who'd rescued Shadow.

"She showed up on our front steps on Christmas Eve. Cutest little thing you've ever seen," the woman gushed.

We checked at house after house. One man said, "I saw the dog you're talking about on Monday evening. She was running down the street like she was being chased by a bear."

No one else had seen her.

"We know she was in good shape just twelve hours ago," Steve assured me.

"It was cold last night," I worried.

We walked up one street and down another. No Shadow.

"Let's take a swing around in the car," Steve suggested when we got back home. We drove—slowly—through the adjacent neighborhoods. I leaned out the passenger window shouting, "Shadow! Shadow!" Nothing.

Our house was two blocks off the nearby arterial, and I must admit, I used up two tissues before we approached home.

I was blowing my nose again as we pulled into our driveway. To our amazement, a flash of black zoomed out of our open garage. The tires squealed as Steve smashed the brake down. I dashed out my car door and scooped up a quivering black ball.

Our Shadow had found her way home.

Because dogs can't talk, we never found out the whole story. Steve is sure the workman who'd made such a fuss over Shadow stole her.

But how did she get away from her abductor? We'll never know.

Steve and I returned to Shadow's rescuers later that day with a potted plant and happy smiles.

In the midst of the worst of times, we received the best of gifts—our family had been reunited.

To *He-who-guided-her-footsteps-home*, I looked up and whispered, "Thank you."

Chapter 17

FOR EIGHT MONTHS WE paid rent on the *little* house. Steve got a couple of pick-up jobs. I completely set up the new Licensure and Certification Department. Began teaching my manager what Licensure and Certification was all about.

We existed.

However, we were being pressured by the bank, "Pay the full down payment (we'd promised to pay *bocooza* bucks originally when we expected a big amount from the sale of our Tacoma house) and finalize the sale. Or move.

What can we do? I worried.

Then, one day Steve found an ad in the *homes for sale* section of the paper advertising a house across the river in New Albany, Indiana. It said, *Builder will finance.*

We checked it out. Liked it. Got our *pending down payment* money back from the builder of our dream house (a small miracle), added what we'd gotten from Steve's last check, and made a deal with the Indiana builder (who Steve ended up working for later).

I boldly called the vice president, told him we were moving to Indiana. That we'd finally been able to buy a house.

"I expect you to pay for our move. It's the least you can do."

He agreed to pay a moving company to *haul the big stuff* and to reimburse us for renting a U-Haul to take care of the rest.

What we could stash in our car, we did—used only three boxes—over and over. (I never counted the number of drives we made *over the river and through the woods* from Kentucky, over the Ohio River, and into Indiana. But it was a bunch.) The rest went into the rental truck. We loaded all one day—decided to unpack the next.

That night it rained twenty-two inches. The truck leaked. We lost about eighteen of our beautiful leather-bound books. And some personal scrapbook pictures.

Funny thing—when Steve was talking to the builder's accountant later he said, "I'm sure glad I saw that ad for the Dove Circle house in the want ads. We really like it."

The man shook his head and said, "No way. We never advertise our houses. Don't have to—they sell like hotcakes."

A miracle? Both Steve and I agree. It had to have been.

Our move was on the first of February. Soon after, we got a letter from old Tacoma friends, Bert and George, who lived in Charlotte, North Carolina.

"Come visit us," they said.

We jumped at the chance.

The drive to North Carolina, through parts of Kentucky we'd not yet visited, Tennessee, the Great Smokies, and finally into Charlotte, was great. I renewed my love of Southern sweet tea (fostered two years before when I'd represented Hillhaven at a national meeting in Charleston, South Carolina).

For five blessed days, we forgot our troubles and pretended we were *regular* people again. They took us to dinner at their country club—a beautiful place that portrayed the grandeur of the Old South. Steve and George went golfing—Steve got a grass-green *Master's* golf cap. Bert and I went out to lunch and shopping.

Bert and George will never know how much that hiatus from our chaotic world meant to us.

When we got back home, we walked into chaos the minute we opened the garage door and entered our family room.

"Someone broke in our house!" Steve yelled. "Look! The TV's gone. The back door's shattered."

"And they've ruined the carpet," I cried. "My brand-new carpet!" I saw thirteen-inch footprints. Everywhere. I knelt down and felt rust-colored Indiana clay. "Still wet!"

But Steve ignored me—ran into the kitchen like a crazy man.

All I could see was the debris from the cupboards and drawers—strewn on the counters and floor. The burglars had trashed the place.

Chapter 17

My husband was frantically looking through the mess on the counter.

Before I could utter a word, Steve let out a yell that I swear must have been heard ten miles away.

"My rings! My rings! They're gone!"

"What rings?" I asked.

"My wedding ring—the one with the five diamonds. The one you bought me *when we were rich and didn't know it*. And my Keyman ring. I left them next to the sink the night before we left for our trip."

"For heaven's sake why?"

"My eczema."

Those two words said it all. Ever since our bad times had begun, Steve had suffered from a terrible rash when he was stressed—mostly on his hands.

Words escaped me. I gave him a big hug—held on longer than usual.

Together we began our inventory of damage and missing items. Thank goodness we'd purchased homeowner's insurance right after we moved in. But we both knew the jewelry wasn't covered—we'd saved money (false economy!) and not scheduled it.

Will I ever be able to buy him another wedding ring? I agonized.

I knew his Keyman Ring couldn't be duplicated. It was a big chunk of gold with a red ruby in the middle—valuable, nostalgic, and irreplaceable. I remembered the night he'd gotten it. We were in San Diego at the Hotel del Coronado, attending the 1966 Allstate Conference of Champions. Steve had just turned thirty-two. I couldn't have been prouder of my dear husband as he received his company's highest honor.

We've arrived! I rejoiced.

But, all these years later, I wonder. *Did either of us take time to thank God*? I fear not.

To this day, Steve is ringless.

Another regret from that period of time surfaced a year later when I got a letter from Bert. She sounded excited. "We'd like to come see you in May. You did say you could get Kentucky Derby tickets didn't you?"

When I explained I couldn't, I got the feeling she thought I *didn't want* to get them.

I know it sounds crazy—I myself was shocked when I found out—but the only way *ordinary* people can get *Derby* tickets is to inherit them. Other than that, you have to pay out-of-site prices, buy corporate space (expensive), or watch from the in-field (which is a rite-of-passage for local college kids).

For almost any other occasion I could—and did on several times—get box tickets. But the Derby? Never!

～

One day that summer—at 5:15 p.m.—I'd just entered the freeway. Out of nowhere, a bright blue Chevy appeared. Crashed into my car. I found myself whirling. My hands were on the steering wheel, but I had no control.

"God help me," I prayed.

Twirling counter-clockwise, my vehicle was facing the wrong direction when I crashed into a Ford Explorer. Tires screeched. A fourth driver joined the melee.

By the time it was all over, four vehicles were stopped, going every-which-way in the midst of five o'clock traffic.

I stood on the side of the freeway. Terrified . . . Afraid I had no insurance . . . (I hadn't paid the premium that month.) Knowing I had out-of-state license plates . . .

The only thing I *had* that was up-to-date was a new Indiana driver's license.

In the confusion, all the police officer asked me for was my driver's license.

Thank you God!

My car limped over the bridge.

Steve was amazed I'd made it home. "Your car is undriveable," he told me. "Thank goodness we have insurance."

I lost it. Cried.

"I didn't pay the premium this month. Maybe they'll give me some leeway."

"You've got to be kidding," he yelled. "All those years working in an insurance agency—and you didn't learn that coverage stops when you don't pay on time?"

"But I didn't have enough money this month," I whined.

"No excuse," he said. "And I hate to tell you this, Darlene, but you've got a worse problem than a wrecked car. They could take away your driver's license for driving a vehicle without insurance."

Chapter 17

That night I worried. Prayed. Worried some more. Began a novena to St. Jude, the patron of lost causes.

The next day I spent my lunch hour on my knees at the Cathedral in downtown Louisville.

It was a long week.

That Saturday, the phone rang. It was the insurance adjustor representing the driver of the Chevy. "The kid's admitted he caused the accident. We'll fix your car. Get you a rental car."

I cried—in happiness. I finished the novena—then said another one of *Thanks*.

My mother had been in an Alzheimer's unit in a Tacoma nursing home for seven years. When we moved, they advised me it wouldn't be good to move her 2,000 miles—even to be near me. It sounded crazy—I was working for a nursing home chain for goodness sake—we had a facility a mile away. They were adamant.

In late August, Stephanie called. "Grandma's bad," she said.

"Call the church. Get her the Last Rites."

Stephanie made the call. Was told, "We go to the nursing home once a month. That's all we do. She's okay."

Mother died on August 30. When I called to make funeral arrangements—at the same church my father had been buried from in 1977—the secretary said, "She doesn't belong to this parish."

"I know that. But we were members for twenty-five years. Before we moved, I called and told you she was in the nursing home—that she was in bad shape. You specifically said there'd be no problem when my mother died."

"Well, we have a different priest now." And different meant, *No funeral unless you're a registered member.*

I was beside myself. *No funeral? That's not fair!*

It certainly wasn't what I'd expected. I was furious.

Steve called. He did no better.

But, thanks to my dear, wonderful Steve, my mother *did* have a funeral—of sorts.

He called the brother of a Gonzaga friend—Father Weber, principal at Bellarmine High School in Tacoma. Father Weber prayed a service for the family at the funeral home and said a Mass for my mother immediately after at the Bellarmine chapel.

Only family attended—Michele and her two sons, Larry and Sean, and Stephanie and her boy Jake. And me. (Steve stayed in Indiana—buying two plane tickets wasn't financially possible.)

My mother, at ninety-one, had outlived everyone but the seven of us.

It was a sad day. There was no gathering of old friends after the funeral. No luncheon given by the church ladies. Just the six of us having lunch at The Ram.

That evening, sitting with my daughter in a candlelit living room, Michele said, "Grandma was a hard woman to love."

I agreed.

We both knew my mother's history—her own mother died when she was three days old. Her father was almost sixty at the time. Her youngest sibling was a thirteen-year-old brother—her oldest, who she almost never saw, was a thirty-year-old husband and father. I know she was well cared for—but loved? Really loved?

My mother never kissed me. I remember when I was about eight and had just spent the night at my friend Helen's house. I'd been surprised when I saw Helen's mother come in, bend over the bed, and give her a big kiss. The next day I asked my mother why she didn't kiss me. She said, "Kisses are full of germs." So much for that.

But my mother was a good woman. A faithful wife for forty-two years, she gave me birth—a home—grandmothered my Michele and Stephanie, enjoyed her three great-grandsons. She did the best she could. She *was* loved.

The timing in my mother's passing gave me pause. Marie Georgia Stroble Barnes left this earth on the same day as Princess Diana. Just six days before Mother Teresa.

Does being a celebrity on Earth have anything to do with our entrance into Heaven? I wondered.

I toyed with a strange thought. *I wonder. Did the three of them—my mother, Princess Diana, and Mother Teresa—sit beside each other at the weekly newcomer's luncheon that first week in September in 1997?* I hope so.

Chapter 17

It was a Saturday morning in early October. I stood in the produce department of Kroger's in New Albany, Indiana—with tears streaming down my face.

The sign in front of my eyes said "Blue Chelan Apples—Washington Grown." I picked up one of the distinctively-shaped Red Delicious apples that brought back so many happy memories, rubbed my index finger over the surface as if polishing it. Broke into sobs—right in the biggest supermarket in southern Indiana.

Steve, who'd been picking out next week's breakfast bananas, saw me and instantly knew my problem.

"You can't keep agonizing about not being able to go to Chelan," he told me, even though I knew he missed the place too.

"I know you loved being right on the lake. A day didn't go by that I didn't see you gazing across the water at *your valley*. There may be peaks higher than Stormy Mountain, but none can be any more majestic. We both enjoyed vacationing there. But that's done with, and you've got to get over it. We don't own the condo any more. You're working in downtown Louisville. We're living in the Hoosier State."

I sobbed all the harder. Life in the South had not turned out the way we'd planned.

But we were both determined to make a new life. In Indiana.

Steve picked up a sack, started putting in apples. Gave me a little hug.

I offered him a weak smile. Added in a couple more apples. We continued our Saturday routine. Together.

Chapter 18

I SUSPECT THE FIRST pains began around October, 1997. But it wasn't until we began planning our Christmas trip to Tacoma that Steve admitted, "I have a little problem."

I sent him to my doctor who listened to his symptoms and prescribed Metamucil. It didn't help. He saw her again—got another over-the-counter prescription. Still no relief.

On his April 1 birthday, I took Steve out—we'd always loved dining at nice restaurants. In the middle of eating, he grabbed his stomach.

"I've gotta leave," he said. I heard agony in his voice.

(After all these years, I wonder—*Did I pay our bill*? At the time, *that* was the least of my worries.)

"I'm fine. Just indigestion," he said an hour later.

But the pains got worse after that—more often. He didn't complain. But while working on the house (we had a half-dozen projects in-process), he'd have to stop—bend over a moment—obviously in pain.

When I suggested going back to the doctor, he said, "It'll go away." And in a minute—or five—it did.

Then—in the middle of the night of April 7—I woke to find Steve looming over me.

"I can't stand it anymore," he gasped. "Please . . . Get me to Emergency. Now!"

Two days of tests and worry later, I got a call from his new, hospital-designated doctor when I was at work. "It's cancer. I'll operate tomorrow," he said with no preamble.

Immediately, I called our church.

"Will you please go to the hospital (it wasn't far) and give Steve a blessing before the operation?" I asked our priest.

"I'm way too busy," he said.

Chapter 18

I couldn't believe what I was hearing—twice in just seven months I'd been denied help! First for my mother—now for Steve.

I was furious! It was all I could do not to look up and say, "I quit!"

But, from somewhere in my depths, I heard a voice say, "Just because that priest isn't doing his job doesn't mean you can stop doing yours. Your job right now is to take care of your husband. Do it!"

I cried. Tears calmed me. Cleansed my soul.

Furtively, I looked around. No one had seen my almost-melt down. I went back to work.

The next day I stopped at the hospital and visited Steve before heading to my office. After working all morning, I walked over to the Cathedral (right across the street from my building) and prayed the Good Friday service in a packed church. Then I drove over the river to the hospital—and waited. And waited. No news.

At 4:30, Maureen, our Butte friend, and Sandy, our Louisiana buddy, arrived to offer support.

Thank God I'm not alone anymore.

An hour later I saw the doctor approaching. I ran to meet him as he came down the corridor.

"It's over," he said. "The tumor was too large for me to take out. So I sewed him back up again. He's in recovery."

You what?" I screamed. "Sewed him up because his tumor was *too big*? What's the poor man supposed to do? He's been in agony. You've got to do something!"

The doctor acted like this had been an ordinary surgery—ignored his phone diagnosis that Steve had cancer.

"We'll observe him," the doctor said as he turned to leave.

That was it!

I was dumbfounded. *How can Steve live?* I agonized. *Pain so bad he can't stand it and all the doctor says is, "Too big!"*

Maureen and Sandy took me to a little restaurant nearby. It was well after six. Everyone was eating dinner. All I could choke down was a sliver of pie.

I went back to the hospital and waited until Steve woke up from the anesthesia. Fussed over him a bit. Went home. Sat in a chair and made the calls I'd avoided before the operation—to our daughters, his mother, his sisters.

After the last call, I broke down and cried, until there were no more tears.

About ten the phone rang.

"I'm here for you," I heard Maureen say.

"I understand," I answered, not really believing anyone could help.

Then she told me *her* story.

"Years ago I had colon cancer myself. I want you to know that I survived. Steve will too."

All of a sudden, a miracle happened. I knew in my heart that Steve would not only survive. He'd thrive.

I can never thank Maureen enough. That night in April she saved me. We talked. I calmed down.

"Call me whenever you need to talk. Day or night," she said. "Now try and get some sleep."

I never called her in the middle of the night. Knowing I *could* was all I needed.

~

The next weeks were sheer hell.

At Steve's after-surgery appointment five days later, the doctor said, "I've decided you have Crohn's disease." He smirked—as if he'd said something profound—like, *Aren't you proud of me discovering what's bothering you?'*

The doctor's idea of encouragement was to say, "My mother has Crohn's, and she's doing fine. You'll live."

How? He didn't say.

Frankly, we were *not* happy. We researched Crohn's disease. First of all, it's incurable. Which means you have to live with the symptoms of abdominal pain (believe me, Steve had *that*), severe diarrhea, fatigue, and weight loss. He'd already dropped from 210 to 190. And finally, sometimes Crohn's leads to life-threatening complications.

"I'd rather have cancer," Steve said. "It'd either beat me, or I'd beat it. Either way I wouldn't have to live with cancer forever."

For two weeks, a home health nurse came every day to swab Steve's incision and change his dressing. I'd tried—once. Removing the giant gauze pad covering the incision, I'd taken a sterile, foot-long Q-tip out of its sealed container and looked down into the hole I was supposed to clean. I felt like

Chapter 18

I was standing at the rim of a volcano—before it exploded—looking into curdling, molten lava. I called for help.

The wound healed. Steve continued losing weight (although I was filling him with oatmeal cookies and lots of good food). The pains continued.

One Saturday morning in late May, when Steve was sitting in his recliner watching TV, and I was working in the kitchen, I heard an ungodly sound. *From Steve?* I watched in horror as he got up and ran to the nearby bathroom.

I followed. Saw a stream of green goo erupt from Steve's incision—just like Mount St. Helens when she blew.

I tried to get the doctor. He was unavailable by phone. Finally I got his *service*. Told them my story.

"Take him to emergency," they said.

"My God, how?" I cried. "I had to strip him—he's covered with gunk."

"Wrap him in a blanket," the voice said just before it hung up on me.

I ran up to the bedroom, got his bathrobe and slippers, rushed back down and wiped him down with a towel as best I could. Then I dressed him.

Twenty minutes later we arrived at Emergency. No one noticed us. I ran to the head of the line of poor souls waiting for service.

"My husband needs help! Now!" I demanded.

Three days later the doctor decided he'd operate. Again.

"And how do you think you'll be able to do better this time?" I asked, unable to keep the sarcasm from my voice. "You failed miserably just six weeks ago."

"I'll have help," the doctor said. "Another surgeon and a urologist."

I wasn't happy. But . . .

This time I did things differently. I got a priest from a neighboring parish who prayed with Steve. I didn't go to work. I got to the hospital early, sat by Steve in his room while he waited, and kissed him as they rolled his bed back to the operating room.

For hours I sat in the huge waiting room praying. "Please God guide the surgeon's knife. Help him get it all. Heal my Steve for me." I prayed rosary after rosary.

Mid-afternoon, Steve's sister Dodo and her husband Ray arrived. They'd flown in from St. Paul. I don't remember when I've ever been so happy to see anyone.

The doctor came, said Steve was doing well, that he would be in recovery a couple of hours

"Time to get out of here for a while. Have some dinner," Ray said. We went to a nice, riverside restaurant. I can't remember what I ate, but I'll never forget Dodo and Ray's very *presence*.

Saturday morning Steve had a terrible story to tell us.

"When I woke up after surgery, I saw a complete stranger sitting at the foot of my bed. Blinked to make sure I was awake and not dreaming. Sure enough, it was a man. He wore a black suit, white shirt, and black tie. His hair was pure white and flowed like he'd just arrived on a plane with an open cockpit.

"I swear, I didn't know if it was *God* come to get me, or the *devil*.

"When he saw me move, the man said, 'Every once in a while we have to tell our patients bad news. You have colon cancer. There'll be a radiologist and an oncologist here to see you.' Then he walked out of the room. Didn't give me a chance to ask a single question. For a minute, I really wondered if I were dead or alive. Then I got to worrying. What does having colon cancer mean? Am I going to die? Soon?"

Dodo, Ray and I were speechless. *What could we say? How could we ease Steve's mind?*

We hugged him. Gingerly—not wanting to hurt our already hurting Steve. Made small talk.

When the nurses arrived soon after, they told us, "The patient needs rest."

Assuring Steve we'd be back, the three of us left. I drove to Fuzzy Zeller's Covered Bridge restaurant where the three of us had a lovely, long lunch. Mid-afternoon we came back to the hospital. Visited with Steve. Went off for dinner. Stopped to tell Steve "good night" on our way to our home on Dove Circle.

Sunday we went to church, out to breakfast, and then stopped at the hospital to see Steve.

Afterwards, Dodo and Ray drove their rented car to the airport, and flew back to St. Paul. Their visit was a lifesaver for me. I'll treasure the memory of their kindness, and their love. Forever.

Chapter 18

Ten days after surgery, Steve had an appointment with the surgeon at his office. I expressed my worry.

"Steve's down to a hundred-forty-three pounds."

"Well, I *did* take a five-pound tumor out of him," the doctor said.

"Big deal! He's lost sixty-eight pounds since December. That's not normal! And what about the chemo and radiology? Will that cause him to lose more?"

"We'll see," said the surgeon. With that, he dismissed us.

Steve and I looked at each other in disgust.

That summer was tough. Steve had both chemo and radiation.

Stephanie and Jake arrived for a ten-day visit. During a regular radiation treatment, Steve's signs turned so bad the doctor put him in the hospital—for a week.

Jake's only fun with Poppa on that trip was seeing him—in his sickbed—at the hospital or later at home. It was hard—they'd been buddies.

On Steve's first visit to the oncologist, the doctor explained the procedure.

"You'll have one treatment a week for twelve weeks," she said. "The drug we'll use—5-Fluorouracil or 5-FU as we commonly call it—has been used for some time. With very good results."

"Heavenly days!" Steve exclaimed. "In 1961, when I worked for Roche Laboratories as a detail man, a hematologist I called on in Spokane, Washington told me, 'I'm using 5-FU as an experimental drug. It wasn't effective in breast cancer, but we're finding it works very well in treating gastrointestinal cancer.'

"Here it's thirty-seven years later, and you're treating me with a drug I used to detail."

"It's the best there is," the oncologist said.

Steve began his treatments. I was amazed when he wouldn't even let me drive him back and forth.

"My boss has no problem with me taking time to chauffeur you," I said.

"No way!" my strong-willed husband said. I was further amazed when, after his first treatment, I came home to find him cooking dinner.

My man is unbelievable! I thought as I sent a quick "thank you" upward.

One day as Steve was waiting to have his chemo treatment, he saw a man come in dressed in a suit, white shirt, and tie. *Detail man*, he thought. Looking closer, he noticed the man's business card affixed to his briefcase. Under his name it said: *Roche*.

The two got to chatting, and Steve told the story of how he'd *detailed* 5-FU in 1961.

"I'm amazed," the salesman said. "I knew 5-Fluorouracil was the drug of choice for colon cancer, but I had no idea it had been around that long."

During those long twelve weeks, Steve's only complaint was, "sitting there—for two hours—is just plain boring."

My job was intense. Our company was in the middle of a REIT (Real Estate Investment Trust). My specific job included change-of-ownership documentation for over 300 facilities. One day—I have no idea what pushed me over the threshold—I made a call I'd been avoiding. I made an appointment with a psychologist.

She listened to my story. About our move from Tacoma to Louisville. My job being immediately downsized. Getting ripped off by the company buy-out of our creek house. About Steve's health problems and ensuing five surgeries—his frustration with not being able to do what he wanted to do. About the stress of my job.

"This is the secret," the analyst said. "Get mad!"

"Get mad?" I shouted. "And what good is *that* going to do?"

She told me a lot of garbly-gook.

"Who do I get mad at? My boss? My poor husband? As if Steve planned on getting sick? As if my boss made the company rules? As if the company cared?"

I left in a huff. Maybe *that* was the therapy.

Nothing changed. Except—slowly—my realization that I needed to change my own attitude.

Maybe things weren't what I'd expected. I wasn't where I'd thought I'd be at this point in my life. Maybe life wasn't fair.

But I *did* have a lot going for me. I straightened my spine and kept walking. Forward.

Chapter 19

STEVE AND I HAD a surprisingly fun summer that very hard year. I made it a point to discover a different place to explore every weekend. Sometimes it might just be a ride through the emerald green farmland on the bench above the area where we lived.

Other times we explored. At Corydon, the site of a Civil War battle, I posed by a cannon. We bought four porcelain bunny napkin holders at a gift shop. At Paoli we found a perfect old-fashioned town square. At French Lick we ate at an old hotel where gangsters from Chicago had stayed while they *took the waters* at nearby West Baden Springs.

But to me, the very best place was only five minutes away—a little family-owned ice cream stand in Sellersburg that served the best chocolate chip ice cream in the whole world (and I must admit, I'm an ice cream expert). We went there often.

One Sunday we drove to Louisville and toured the newly redone Speed Art Museum that was featuring the Wyeths—father Jamie, daughter, and son Andrew. My very favorite section was *The Helga Pictures*. In *Braids* I counted the strands of hair in her thick plaits. In *Sheepskin,* the whorls in the fabric looked so real it was as if I'd touched the painting and felt soft fleece. Steve had to drag me away.

Finally the REIT was done! I have to admit, there were times when I thought I'd never be able to send that very last change-of-ownership package off. For some states, the documentation for just one facility measured twelve inches thick. We had 350 to document.

While the company employed over 1,200 people at the corporate office in downtown Louisville, only twenty-two actually worked on the project.

To celebrate, Steve and I had lunch at Fuzzy Zeller's restaurant. We ate on the patio. I loved watching the golfers putt on the eighteenth green while I sipped sweet iced tea—one of my favorite things.

"Done is done!" I told Steve while lifting my glass as it were a crystal flute of champagne.

"Amen," he answered.

Imagine my surprise the next Monday when I got an invitation from the company president to celebrate the completion of the REIT—at Churchill Downs.

The day came—we were treated royally. Guided to the President's Suite, we found a large, sumptuous area decorated in an equestrian decor. French doors beckoned onto a wrought iron balcony with a bird's-eye view of the paddock.

Up until my move to Louisville, my love affair with horse racing was more Valley County Fair than Kentucky Derby. That day I felt as if I were Abe Lincoln, transported from my childhood log cabin to the White House.

Wandering around, gazing at the portraits, admiring the horses, I almost ran into the white-haired legend of horse racing—Bob Baffert.

I'd arrived in Louisville on April 26, 1996. A few days later, on May 4, I'd watched on TV as Baffert's horse Cavonnier came in a close second in the Kentucky Derby. It just took that one race to get me hooked.

The next two years, Baffert's horses—Silver Charm in 1997 and Real Quiet in 1998—won not only the Derby but also the Preakness and placed second in the Belmont.

Now I heard him say, "My name's Bob Baffert. So glad you meet you."

We chatted about horse racing and the Derby and Louisville for at least ten minutes. When we parted, Baffert said, "I'd appreciate if you'd put in a good word for me with Bruce (our company CEO and President). I'd love to train one of his horses."

(Like I had Bruce's ear! I smiled to myself.)

The rest of the afternoon was a fog of fun. We could see the horses and their jockeys walk around the paddock before a race and go across the hall and watch the race in the grandstand. They had betting machines in the suite, but I chose to go right up to the main window and turn over my two dollars on each of the races. (Came out even.)

All afternoon we were wined and dined. The best wine. Shrimp so big each one seemed like a meal. I don't have enough time or room here to mention all the delicacies.

Chapter 19

To this day, I love to tell the story of my most memorable afternoon in Louisville and my visit with Bob Baffert. I never miss watching the Kentucky Derby on the first Saturday of May. (In 2015, I watched Baffert's horse American Pharaoh win both the Derby and the Preakness. And then, by winning the Belmont in a wire to wire race, be awarded the jewel of racing—the American Triple Crown. *Wow!*)

In August of that year, Steve's family had a reunion in Yellowstone Park. Steve said, "No. Too expensive." Our kids sent us tickets—we got the message.

We started in Butte, toured Yellowstone on a private fifty-person bus, spending a night at each of four hotels. Both of our daughters came, bringing their children—our three grandsons. Dodo arrived with Ray and her three children. Steve's sister Sis and her four kids were there—Sis's son-in-law Steve owned and drove the bus. And special guest was Steve's mother.

Pictures viewed later showed an emaciated Steve. I remember one time he could hardly walk up a small hill. But he had heart. We didn't miss a thing.

It was a perfect way to enjoy our extended family. Thank you Michele and Stephanie for forcing us to go.

1999

I worked with some wonderful people in Louisville. Like Maureen who in 2006 came to our Fiftieth Wedding Anniversary in Tacoma from her new home in Denver.

And Shirley who was one of my first hires. Shirley flew to Washington State twice to visit—alone when we lived in Chelan, then with her new husband Bob during our first segment in Wenatchee. And who's planning to make a third trip as I'm writing this book.

During our years in the South, someone was always visiting. Stephanie and Jake came at least eight times. The first summer, Michele sent Larry and Sean alone on the plane. The last August we were there, Michele and the boys visited.

In 1999, we had lots of company. Glasgow—Phyllis and Bill from Kalispell—Jennie and Bob from Iowa.

Karen and Gary—Tacoma friends we'd first met in 1966. Karen and I had been amazed when we found out how much we had in common—we were both married on August 18, 1956—in Montana (Glasgow for us—Billings for the Fowlers).

Early in the year we got a letter from Spokane friends, Helen and Bob Durgan.

"This September we're exchanging a week of our Florida time-share for a golf vacation at French Lick in Southern Indiana. On the map it looks like it's in your backyard," Helen wrote. "Bob and I'd love to have you come up and see us while we're there. We're bringing Jack (McKenna)."

Thus, one warm, humid September Sunday night, we found ourselves at the French Lick Country Club having dinner with three college friends. I sat next to Jack, newly widowed, an obstetrician who'd known Steve since they were both twenty and in chemistry class at Gonzaga together. After dinner and lots of talk, Jack took me aside and said, "Did you realize Steve's suffering from depression?"

I choked a bit. Jack was an obstetrician, not a psychiatrist.

Seeing my surprise, he said, "That's common for cancer patients, Darlene. What he needs is a change of pace."

On the trip back home that evening, I thought, *It wasn't an accident Jack happened to vacation thirty miles from our house. God's trying to tell me something.*

Steve and I had already talked about moving back to Tacoma to be closer to our family. I'd balked. *I had an important job for heaven's sake!*

My talk with Jack was secret. But I started watching Steve. Thinking.

When you get a message out of the blue, it's time to take notice.

By October we'd made the decision to move back to Tacoma. I'd been unhappy about the business path my company was taking. Steve had never found his niche in the South.

We cashed in a retirement account to pay for our move (not company-paid this time around).

Our kids were ecstatic. Steve loaded up his car with what was left of our leather-bound books and all his clothes. He drove back to Tacoma where he lived with Stephanie—temporarily.

At Thanksgiving, I flew to Tacoma. We found a house. I put our Indiana property up for sale and started checking out jobs in the Tacoma area. Steve arranged the new house deal. He'd gotten his long dormant teacher's certificate renewed and was substitute teaching. We moved forward.

Chapter 19

I returned for a week at Christmas when I began job hunting for real. I interviewed with possible employers from Gig Harbor to downtown Seattle.

One morning, while reading the front page of the *Tacoma News Tribune*, Steve announced, "There's a new company in town called Total Renal Care. The paper says they're hiring *anything warm.*"

"I'm a little more than *warm*," I fussed. But I checked out the company. Found that an old friend was already working there. The day I met with her, personnel posted a new job: Supervisor-Licensure and Certification. I applied.

No sooner had I gotten back to work in Louisville than I got a call from the director of Total Renal Care. He wanted to fly me back to Tacoma for an interview.

I took a Friday off, flew out of Louisville at dawn, arrived by cab (they'd had it meet me at the airport) just before 1 p.m., and spent the entire afternoon interviewing.

First I met with the director for an hour. Next came the manager. Then several staff members. Finally I was introduced to the vice president.

It seemed I was perfect for them. A national renal dialysis company, they were just setting up their Licensure and Certification department. That's what I'd done in Louisville.

I gave a four week notice and began planning.

As I sorted through our possessions in preparation for the movers, I spent some time soul searching.

Steve and I had come to the South excited about beginning again. But . . .

We should never have sold Matule Insurance. It was Steve's life.

Sure, our business had had a little hiccup. But, instead of taking a spoon of sugar, we'd cut off its head.

The travel agency we retired into *turned into a money pit. We stayed for two years. Bad mistake!*

Steve's non-compete agreement with the buyer of our agency prevented him from doing what he really liked—running his own insurance business. He ended up being an order taker. *And not enjoying it one bit.*

Within six weeks of arriving in Louisville, we'd had our expectations dashed. Our house deal proved to be a disaster. Steve's place with a local insurance agency (negotiated in March when we'd come house hunting) disintegrated. My job turned into a sham of what had been promised.

We could have given up. (I shudder as to what that would have entailed.) But we stayed put. Got up every morning. Kept working—not at what we'd expected. But working.

During one of my hardest days in Louisville I wrote the following affirmation. Printed it. Posted it on the wall right above my computer. It kept me going on my job for four years. Now I read it often in my current *Affirmation Notebook*.

I believe I am always divinely guided.
I believe I will always be led to take the right turn in the road.
I believe that God will always make a way where there is no way.

In the years since we left the South, Steve and I have often said:

"Those four years were . . .
the Worst of Times
and
the Best of Times."

And they were.

Chapter 20

WHEN WE LEFT SPOKANE in 1966, we moved to Tacoma. To a subdivision called Oakbrook. But even then, it had been part of a greater area called Lakewood.

By the time we moved back in 2000, the area had been incorporated—even had a city hall.

Since we knew the area, we decided to look it over ourselves to find what was for sale.

On the first day, while taking a short cut, we drove past a long ranch house on Huggins Meyer Road. We got out and walked the perimeter. Liked what we saw. It was offered by Apple Real Estate.

"Synchronicity again." I said. (It seemed to be following us.) "Apples are us."

How could it not be? What could be more fortuitous than this?

Steve called his Rotary friend Ron who met us on site. Inside we found a forty-year-old house that had been rented out for thirty years. The floors were a mess—original oak had apparently been carpeted—now bare, it showed the result of letting dogs *do-their-business* inside. The wood was etched with urine—past being saved by sanding. It looked like the walls hadn't been painted for thirty-five years. The tile in two bathrooms was dated. The basin in the third must have been a heroin *cook site*—the porcelain looked like it had a terminal case of leprosy. The yard was overgrown.

We loved it.

Ron showed us more houses. Dupont—new, nice. Oakbrook (a block and a half from our first home)—small, dated.

Shaking his head at our choice, Ron sold us the first house. Unfortunately he had a heart attack right after and never got to see what we did with the place.

Similar to the floorplan of our creek house, it had pluses that one didn't—bigger living, dining, and family rooms—a bedroom-sized den connected by a double arch to the master—a much bigger attached garage complete with a wall of floor-to-ceiling cabinets. Plus a separate garden-garage.

Steve sanded old wainscoting in the family room and kitchen. We both scraped off several layers of wallpaper. He re-finished the kitchen cabinets (they looked beautiful when he was done!). We painted (Steve was boss—I was go-fer). We papered (I was boss—Steve was go-fer). We added a solid oak mantle to the family room fireplace and embellishments to the one in the living room. The doors were good quality—solid core—but stained. We painted them white and replaced the woodwork with new molding—also painted white.

We added new carpeting and vinyl throughout. Put in all new windows. And best of all, installed a brilliant white, flawless pedestal sink in the third bath.

I made lined draw drapes for the master and den, swag window treatments for the living and dining rooms, and cornices over white, eyelet-edged curtains for the two other bedrooms. We had 20 sky-high Douglas firs removed from the front and side yards. Steve tore out a hillside of ivy-gone-mad. We bought tons of new plants and planted them.

We had fun!

My work was challenging. I worked with some great people. Hired more. Added hundreds of new dialysis facilities nationwide. Developed a state-of-the-art filing system using the expertise I'd perfected while on the job in Louisville. Introduced things like *Bear Town* and *Shop 'n Talk* at Christmas to liven department friendships.

Steve began substitute teaching. Changed jobs. Became a Knights of Columbus insurance representative.

We were five minutes from each of our daughter's homes.

We renewed old friendships and made new ones.

Life was good.

Steve had a previous habit of giving me expensive Christmas presents: a mink stole, a string of pearls, a Grandfather clock.

Chapter 20

I'd reciprocated with less expensive, but very personal gifts—like our much-loved Shadow. Another year I gave him my one and only poem. It began:

Shadow
Like a Christmas Star
She blazed into my life.
A jet black ball of fur
Soft as well-washed corduroy,
With a heartbeat
That joined my own.

Shadow spent fifteen happy Christmases with our family.

Then, a surprise. We were offered a week's condo stay in Chelan in mid-January. We snapped it up! Quick.

As usual when we were in Chelan, Steve went to the Tuesday Rotary lunch meeting. While there, he met a man from our old Oakbrook neighborhood who was now selling financial services through a local bank. "They're looking to add an insurance agency," Dewey said, "Interested?"

It makes no sense, I told myself. We had a great thing going for us in our Huggins Meyer Lakewood house—new jobs, proximity to our family.

Yet, it made all the sense in the world—how many times had I lamented when Friday morning got there and our condo stay ended at noon? Once Steve had asked, "How long do you think you could stay in Chelan without getting bored?" I honestly couldn't answer him.

Steve quit his job and rented a condo by-the-month. To try things out.

In February I took a week of vacation (I had five) and enjoyed living in the luxury condo with Steve. We started looking around.

In March I took a long weekend, and we looked at houses.

I went up for another four-day weekend in May. We did some serious house looking. I'll never forget the Saturday we found *the perfect house*.

Looking back, I realize the realtor had figured me out—I was looking for a view. He hurried me through the needs-a-lot-of-tender-loving-care house to the side-deck off the kitchen.

Wow!

Before me I saw the Chelan golf course, the town, and mountains in the distance. Not waiting for the mood to disappear, he led me around the corner to a house-long deck.

Another *Wow!*

Here—for a 180 degrees of unobstructed view—I saw the shimmering water of Lake Chelan. I felt as if I were in heaven.

We immediately made an offer.

When we got back to the rental condo, the phone was ringing. It was our grandson Larry. He'd just found out that he'd gotten a four-year scholarship to Gonzaga.

What a day!

I went back to Lakewood and put our house up for sale. It sold—for the asking price—in thirty days.

Ron's son was our real estate agent. He'd seen what bad shape the house was in when we bought it. I remember him telling me just before we moved, "You did a super job updating this place. It looks like something from *House Beautiful*."

I basked in the compliment.

We had to vacate by July 1. No problem—our Chelan place closed the end of May. Steve moved in.

But there *was* a problem. I hadn't quit my job. Hadn't even told my company I was thinking of moving. (I loved that job.)

I thought, *One thing at a time.*

In the month of June, I worked every day at my downtown Tacoma job, came home and packed at night, and, in my spare time, found a one-bedroom apartment in Steilacoom to tide me over.

The Fourth of July was on Thursday that year—I took the whole week as vacation. The movers came on June 28 and loaded the big stuff.

Steve moved the basics—mattress and box spring, one loveseat, a couple of lamps, my sewing machine, computer, our library table (I'd use it to eat on), one extra chair, and selected clothes to my apartment the next day. Then he started filling the U-Haul we'd rented with the small *stuff* I'd packed for Chelan. We slept on the *bed-on-the floor* in the Steilacoom apartment that Saturday night.

On Sunday, June 30, we finished loading the rental truck, completed cleaning our sold house, and slept in our own bed in Chelan that night.

I was in limbo. Real job in downtown Tacoma. Real house in Chelan.

Chapter 21

I WORKED LIKE A slave all week unpacking. But I must say, I loved relaxing on our deck every evening with my dear husband.

Life was good.

I went back to my Tacoma job. My Steilacoom apartment.

Then one Sunday when Steve visited me for the weekend at the Steilacoom apartment, disaster struck while we attended church.

During the service, we heard a little gurgle. Looked. Saw the front of Steve's light blue shirt turn navy.

Wet? How?

We left in haste. Found a seam of his colon cancer operation had burst.

The next few days are a blur. Somehow Steve got back to Chelan where he saw Dr. Gordon Tagge who scheduled a PET scan at the University of Washington. Scan done, we waited—Steve in Chelan—me in Tacoma/Steilacoom.

I tried to live normally. *Yeah, right!*

That Friday night I heard a knock at my apartment door.

Who can it be? No one knocks at night, I worried.

"Mom! Mom! It's Stephanie."

When I opened the door, she enfolded me in her arms and whispered, "It's cancer, Mom. The cancer is back."

Early the next morning Stephanie, Jake, and I went to Chelan. Stephanie (bless her!) drove. We showered Steve with kisses, afraid to hug him.

Another blur . . .

I took sick leave to be with Steve during his surgery. When the anesthesiologist asked during pre-op, "And how many surgeries have you had, Mr. Matule?" Steve blinked. Laughed. Said, "Too many!"

Thank God he still has his sense of humor, I thought as I sent up a prayer of thanks.

The surgery was long. I hardly recognized Dr. Tagge as he approached afterwards. His color reminded me of my father's—right after he died. His shoulders were slumped—as if he were Christ carrying His cross. Taking off the little circle-of-gathered-blue he'd worn in the operating room, the doctor hand-combed his hair—just like a swimmer doffing his cap after winning a hard-fought 1500 freestyle race.

I waited...

Finally he said, "Steve's fine. Just fine. The radiation he had after the original colon cancer surgeries fried his small intestines. But I worked hard. Got all the new cancer cells."

Then the doctor did something unheard of in my experience with post-op doctors. He asked me, "And how are you?"

Right then I began blessing Dr. Tagge daily in my prayers. For his expertise—and his kindness.

Steve was in terrible pain—worse than I'd ever seen.

Then—four days later—he perked up. Was released and went home to a quick recovery. He was back at work two weeks later. My husband is amazing.

I finally gave notice—November 29 would be my last day. They offered me continuing employment—in Chelan—working off-site as a Licensure & Certification Specialist. I said a silent, *Thank you Lord! You've given me the best of both worlds!*

That first Christmas we lived in Chelan, we spent the holiday in Tacoma. When I opened my Christmas package from Steve, I found a miniature wooden box filled with perfect Gala apples, my favorite. I thanked him profusely.

"You remembered," I whispered as I gave him a quick kiss.

"No, no," he said. "You missed the point. Look closer!" he urged, pointing to a particular apple.

Chapter 21

I looked. There, tucked between two perfect spheres, I saw a small gold box. Opening it I found a gold apple pendant on a delicate golden chain, lying on a pillow of white satin.

I gasped.

Steve's surprises that Christmas continued. I also found, written on Washington apple stationery, a handwritten note from a man who knew me well. A man who had loved me through good times and bad alike.

The note said:

You never *have to be without a Chelan apple* ever *again.*

I cried. The best kind of tears—tears of happiness.

Now, each time I wear my beautiful *Apple*, I feel Christmas love enfold me.

My life is indeed blessed!

Forty-seven years, three months, four days from when my husband Steve first touched my shoulder and asked, "Wanna dance?" I opened my curbside mailbox and retrieved a three-by-three-by-one inch box.

Noting my sister-in-law's return address, I opened it to find Rod Stewart encased in plastic.

"My God!" I shouted loud enough to be heard three counties away, "Dorothy Jean's gone mad!"

Now, I've got to tell you, of all the Rock & Roll singers I might have considered leaving my husband for in the seventies and eighties, Rod Stewart was at the bottom of my list.

But when Steve came home, Rod did his magic. The two of us danced—like new lovers—to the strains of *I'm in the Mood for Love*. Right in our kitchen.

We both ended up loving Rod Stewart's *The Great American Songbook* so much we bought the sequel as soon as it came out. We've been dancing to Rod's unique voice as he sings our favorites—like *Let's Fall in Love* and *Thanks for the Memory*—ever since.

We both loved Chelan. In the summer I'd bring my work outside as often as I could. Imagine, being paid for editing—while basking in the splendor of Lake Chelan.

Steve thrived in his job—met lots of interesting people.

Our new house was outdated so we did it over completely. The old garage became a lovely family room. Every wall surface was either papered or painted. I did the kitchen and family room both with a faux finish—kitchen-shades of blue—family room-shades of beige. Steve and I put up borders—bunnies in the kitchen, ducks in the family room. We had new counters installed in the kitchen. Steve painted the cabinets a bright white—making it my favorite kitchen of all time. For a finale we had hardwood installed in the hallways.

We hired professionals for two outside jobs—to paint the siding and to install a rock waterfall and koi pond.

Steve and I dug out and disposed of the sagebrush that surrounded our property—to protect our house from burning in case of a brush fire. (Later, when a fire was stopped one hill from our place, a fire fighter told Steve, "You guys did a good job of fire-proofing your property."

We created a series of gardens—front, back, and off the kitchen. If I do say so myself, by the time we were done, we'd turned a desert into an oasis.

I had a three-mile route I walked every Monday through Friday morning. One day, about a half block from home, I felt something strangely squishy under my right foot. Looking down I saw a rattlesnake. Thank goodness someone else had already driven over it, and I'd grown used to living at the edge of civilization.

Having a house located on the highest residential street in Chelan provided a spectacular view as I wound up and down the hill. Sometimes, going home, it felt like I was ascending up to heaven. My spiritual life was enhanced as I walked for exercise.

Steve's Rotary group did *dine around* dinners which were lots of fun. We cooked for new friends—ate tasty cuisine with others at their homes.

We became active at St. Francis de Sales Church. One year I supplied the Grand Raffle prize item for their annual bazaar—a 16-inch doll with a complete handmade wardrobe—from ball gown to play clothes to (my favorite) a bright red wool coat worn over a winter white dress. It made my women's group almost $900. The next year Steve had the winning ticket and won an oak table lamp with a professionally-crafted stained-glass shade.

Chapter 21

As soon as the leaves on our backyard apricot tree began turning color, Steve and I came up with the same idea. *We need a new Christmas Castle!* Seven years had been entirely too long to be without our much-loved decoration.

Steve set up shop in our ample work room. Before starting, we decided two things. It would be a bit smaller (storage had been a problem, even in our big Creek House), and we'd spare no expense on the finished product.

Using the lessons he'd learned in constructing the first two castles, Steve made this edition even better. The parquet floor gleamed, and the stucco looked professional as did the inside wall coverings. Faux snow outside set the mood for landscaping—a forest of miniature evergreen trees—on either side of the castle. We found a nine-inch golden angel who blew her trumpet while she *floated* above the new castle.

I scoured Christmas shops and found some lovely ceramic mouse miniatures—skaters wearing tiny silver skates, a pianist who sat on the red-velvet bench in front of the baby-grand piano, an acrobat who seemingly climbed up a ceramic tree filled with the teeniest of ornaments.

Fantasy was fun again at the Matule home during December.

I met Patricia Clark at a High Tea she hosted. She was a founding member of the Wenatchee Valley Writers Group and generously sponsored me for membership in October 2003. In July 2005 my first novel, *Under the Gallus Frame*, was published. I will be forever grateful to my friend Patricia.

Our Wenatchee Valley Writers Group met twice a month—on Fridays. Because the Chelan grocery stores tacked an extra 10 percent *tourist* charge on the items they sold, I always stopped at the Wenatchee Albertsons to stock up on essentials on my way home.

Trouble at the Tunnel

One Friday evening in January I approached the Washington Highway 97A tunnel at 6:15 p.m.—well after dark. While it had been snowing when I drove down to Wenatchee that morning, by evening the road was clear. Steve was expecting me home in a half hour—I could almost smell the tasty meal I knew he'd have ready for my arrival.

Driving south from Chelan that morning, I'd made my way through the long, dark, cave-like space that had been blasted out of solid rock.

Staying as close to the hillside as could, I wound down the hill to the flat road below—not too difficult for my acrophobic mind to process.

Coming back from Wenatchee, the approach is on the cliff side—the tunnel so high that I literally prayed myself up when I drove it in the daylight.

At night it's easier. That night I wasn't praying.

Suddenly, as I made the final turn and headed straight to the entrance, a huge rock broke off the mountain. I saw it coming directly at my car. Oblivion hid in the dark to my right. Thank goodness no one was coming the other way.

I jerked the steering wheel left. Then I prayed.

Too late. The boulder hit my front left wheel. It bounced, then attacked the back. My car was still moving forward—barely.

What do I do? I agonized.

Glancing to my right, I saw a black abyss. Still no one coming either way.

Keep calm, I told myself. *Get through the tunnel. There's a turnoff at the other end.*

I pressed the gas. My car limped ahead. The tunnel amplified every groan of my wounded vehicle.

Making my goal, I turned off the ignition. Breathed.

Now what? I asked myself.

No problem, I answered. *Call Steve on your cell phone.*

I pushed my *Favorite Number 1*—Steve.

No ring sound. (I'd forgotten I had mountains on three sides of me, that cell phones can't penetrate solid rock.)

I called again and again. Finally, reality set in. I checked my watch—it's 6:25.

How do I turn on my flashers?

I got out my instruction book—checked the index—read the directions. Finally, success.

This is a busy road, I told myself. *Someone will stop and help. Soon.*

I got excited every time I saw car lights approach. But no one stopped.

The January frost invaded like an enemy. My tummy felt like I was pulling myself through the snow—like a soldier on patrol. I pulled the zipper on my jacket up to the tippy-top. Waited.

What I was really hoping for was a sheriff or state patrol car. I could trust them. *Could I trust just anyone?*

Chapter 21

Dozens of cars passed. Coming... Going... Still, no one stopped.

I kept checking my watch. Checked again—it showed 6:55.

Opening my car door, I got out to check out the terrain. Sinking into the new snow, I realized I'd neglected to wear my snow boots.

Looking around, it seemed as if was at the edge of a cliff. I stopped. Considered walking at the edge of the highway to civilization. I saw no lights ahead—knew the nearest business was Pat and Mike's gas station, miles away. My big toes felt like ice cubes.

Getting back in, I started the engine. Set the heater on high. Just for a few minutes. I started to worry I'd run out of gas.

I prayed the rosary using my fingers as beads. Our Father. Ten digits—the Hail Mary ten times. Repeat, repeat, repeat.

No sheriff. No state patrol. Lots of cars. No one stopped. I honked. No one cared.

I checked my watch. 7:34... 8:00...

At 8:10 a van slowed, came to a stop behind my car. A burly Hispanic man approached. I told him my story. He offered to bring me home. I saw his wife in the front seat and a couple of kids in the back. I said a little prayer and got in.

On the road I began calling Steve. *No service. No service.*

Finally I got a ring tone. Steve answered. He was out looking for me—was almost to the tunnel. We must have passed each other.

My new friends bought me home. They wouldn't take any money, but they did give me their address in Manson. (I'd make it good with them later.)

I watched out the window. Finally I saw lights. It's Steve! I don't know when I've ever been so happy to see him. We hugged. Had a glass of wine. Another. Ate a cold dinner. Cuddled.

The next day, the emergency service of our insurance company got a tow truck to bring our car to town. After getting one new rim and four new tires, our Subaru was good to go.

We checked out the turnoff by the tunnel later. It's just a guess—we didn't measure. But Steve figured if I'd have walked forward six more feet, I'd have fallen down the mountain—it was a shear drop—hundreds of feet down.

Sixty Shades of Love

Trouble in Town

Then a couple of things happened that changed things.

First—we were invaded by packrats.

Steve has always accused me of being a packrat. I tend to save things—just in case. He throws out good stuff—to my chagrin. No more! Once you live with them you never—ever—call anyone a packrat. Even in jest.

It started with a gnawing, particularly annoying smell coming from under our kitchen sink. A smell that wouldn't go away no matter how thoroughly I cleaned or how much Lysol I sprayed.

I'd heard scratching noises coming from our master bath during the night. "Your imagination," said Steve (at a time when his hearing was going from bad to worse).

Then scratching started in daylight. In the laundry room while I was ironing. In our walk-in closet. We found suspicious brownish piles here and there.

The smell got worse. Once we came home after visiting our kids for a few days in Tacoma to find the house smelling so bad we had to open all the windows and doors.

Our bedroom was the worst. For three weeks we had to sleep in the guest room.

Finally Steve admitted—we had alien creatures living with us. He began looking for the source of the scratching and the stench. Following his nose, he found that our furnace was so packed with assorted junk it was a fire hazard.

We called in exterminators.

"You have a full-blown packrat infestation," they told us. "Packrat urine, or midden we call it when we find large, old deposits, is so potent that archeologists use it to date ancient explorations.

"Your packrats have been busy for a long time. Even getting get rid of the current colony of varmints won't help. You'll have to replace your entire furnace duct work system to permanently remove the stink."

It cost us a bundle.

Months after, when Steve had his pickup serviced, the technician said, "Look at this mess." The filter was completely caked with packrat debris.

"Damned packrats!" Steve complained. I emphatically agreed.

Chapter 21

Second—Soon after, the bank decided they didn't want an insurance agency as a subsidiary after all. Steve was without a job.

I was still working. We cut back. Survived.

We loved living in Chelan. It was not on our agenda to leave.

From time to time we invaded our savings.

Then my company moved the Licensure & Certification Department to Memphis, Tennessee. Terminated off-site units like mine.

We began looking around. Found our house had greatly increased in value. We'd added a lot of physical improvements and even more sweat equity. And—the economy was skyrocketing. But finding something in Chelan, even a bit smaller and with a lesser view, cost more than we were willing to pay.

One Sunday, I suggested, "How about Wenatchee?" We made a trip down and were amazed at what we could get for our money.

We listed our house—it sold in six days—at just shy of our asking price. We were both delighted and devastated. We loved Chelan, our breathtaking view, the house we had rebuilt after years of neglect by the former owners.

The buyer gave us ten days to move. I got a cold to end all colds, but couldn't stop working. We had a tight deadline.

To meet the buyer's demands, we had just one day at the end to do what normally would have taken three.

The movers loaded the big stuff.

We then had to pack the U-Haul with the small stuff (we had boxes packed to the ceiling in places).

And the place had to be spotless. (I prided myself in leaving a house cleaner that it had ever been while we lived there.) Since Steve had to be at the new place to let the movers in, that left all the cleaning to me.

I remember fighting with Dish Phone Man that afternoon. We'd completed our contract agreement with them a month before. Knew we'd be moving, so didn't renew—had the document to prove it.

But Phone Man argued, "You have a continuous contract—it'll cost you $500! I won't turn your service off without the money!"

After a trip downtown (to FAX my release paper—not pay), I finally won. But with a physical price. I was zonked—had to lie flat on my back on the living room carpet to get enough energy to finish the cleaning.

It was a tough day.

I drove to our new home—my car stuffed to the seams with *stuff*—at dinner time. Dear Steve had ordered pizza. Bought a bottle of special wine. And my favorite ice cream—chocolate chip.

Perfect.

But... We had great memories of our almost five years living full-time in Chelan. All this time later, I can still close my eyes, think *Chelan,* and be transported to my personal taste of heaven on earth.

Just that March Steve had taken several photos of our fabulous view from the family room. (We didn't have a fancy camera, and I wanted a 180 degree picture.) I spliced the best two together in a scrapbook I planned to put on my coffee table.

Underneath I added the following:

> *This place, 144 Long Drive in Chelan, is a gift.*
> *These words came to me as I sat eating*
> *In my "favorite" kitchen of all time, a blue and white paradise.*
> *I inhaled the sight of snow blanketing "My Valley."*
> *I've learned since, even if a gift's not "forever" perfect...*
> *You don't need to give it back.*
> *You make it your own. Especially after you've moved on.*

Chapter 22

SOON AFTER, ONE OF my friends and I decided to go to Spokane to attend a talk at the Spokane Center for the Arts. I called my eighth grade teacher—Sister Dorothy—to see if she was available to go to either breakfast or lunch with us.

I wasn't surprised when she was busy. Sister explained, "Oh, I'd love to. But I've just started a new job at Sacred Heart Hospital. I'm a receptionist." (She was 87 at the time.) Sister Dorothy had always been a dynamo.

When I got home, I began thinking about Sister Dorothy and what a big part of my life she'd been.

⁓

Sometimes you have to be well past your youth before the enormity of events that happened when you were a kid sinks in.

I know now—eighth grade in St. Raphael's School changed my life—something I'd never have guessed on the first day.

Our brand new school wasn't quite finished on September 6, 1949. For the first four days, classes met in the lunchroom.

Seventh and eighth grades were in the same room. Four girls and sixteen boys comprised our class. Sixteen more rambunctious students were in the seventh. Three of these boys were assigned by the Valley County District Court—*incorrigibles* they called them.

Judge Shea had placed the problem children in our school saying, "No one else has been able to do anything with them. I'm counting on a miracle from the nuns."

But, as I've come to believe over the years, the quality of a school is not determined by bricks and mortar. Or the ratio of students to teacher. The key component of a good education is a special teacher.

Sister Dolores (as we called her in those pre-Vatican II days) was young—not quite twenty-six we learned much later. Relatively inexperienced—she'd only taught three years previously. She had the barest essentials the first two weeks—no books—no desks.

Yet . . . She was, without a doubt, the epitome of teachers.

What makes a "best" teacher?

The title is not the result of being outstanding in one aspect of teaching.

It wasn't the math, or English, or social studies, or history she taught (although she presented each thoroughly and gave us insight that we hadn't gotten the previous seven years).

It wasn't even the extra things—having us memorize the Gettysburg Address or Paul's First Epistle to the Corinthians 13:4-13—"Love is patient; love is kind." It wasn't debates with my childhood pal, Jere. Or even being the angel in the Christmas play.

I struggled with an answer to my question

In the beginning, we were *very* undisciplined, even the best of us. The nuns expected "Yes, Sister. No, Sister. Good morning, Sister." No less. No prior teacher had required such careful manners.

When Johnny, one of the incorrigibles, tried to comply, it sounded more like, "Yes, Stir. No, Stir. Good morning, Stir." But he said it with respect. Sister Dolores accepted his attempt.

Having been taught discipline, we learned respect.

That year St. Raphael's put on an operetta—a completely new experience. Sister Charlotte Marie, the superior, was in charge of singing—my best friend Rita was the star. Sister Dolores was in charge of costumes and sets—I was on her crew. Everyone did something. All of us were complimented. We felt appreciated. Our parents loved our presentations.

Having been taught that everyone has talents—and learning what ours were—we had fun.

After an hour-long lunch, our dual-class needed time to calm down. Sister Dolores knew, and countered our excess energy by spending fifteen minutes each day reading a book out loud. She had a knack of always picking something the entire class enjoyed.

Chapter 22

One day during lunch, someone (I never knew who) put a huge dead owl directly on her chair.

We all knew it was there. No one warned her.

Sister came back, took her book from her desk, pulled out the chair, and sat down without looking.

We waited. For what seemed like hours.

Sister finally rose and shook her hips to remove the offending feathers from the skirt of her full-length black habit. She looked over the room, made eye contact with each of us.

Guilt, in various degrees, invaded each of our hearts.

"Whoever is responsible for this carcass, take care of it. I'm leaving."

Her cheeks were bright red, but she never yelled. She *did* bang the door on the way out.

For a couple of minutes, we were shocked into silence. Then we all started talking at once. We knew we were in big trouble.

Finally we decided what to do.

First of all, the boys united and got rid of all remnants of the dead owl.

Then we chose Gail, the nicest boy in the room who never got in trouble, to be our intermediary.

"Find her," we told him. "Beg if you have to."

I knew Gail well. That minute he looked to me like he'd just as soon jump in the front of a Great Northern freight train as do what we asked him to do. But he went. Stoically.

He was gone a long time.

"She's *real* unhappy," he told us when he returned.

Still we waited.

What will she do? I wondered, knowing we deserved the worst.

When she finally came back, she stood in front of the class like a judge ready to deliver a "guilty" verdict in a murder trial.

"Take out paper—a lot—and a sharp pencil. Start copying this." She wrote a half-dozen sample "I'm sorry" sentences on the blackboard. "Don't stop until I tell you. And use your best penmanship. Sign your name to each page you finish. I guarantee you, I'll check every single sheet handed in."

She calmly sat down at her desk and began reading a book.

We wrote until the bell rang at 4 p.m.

So—what did we learn? Life lessons we never forgot: when and how to retreat, how to admit being wrong—with grace, how to make a personal commitment never to fall off the straight and narrow again.

Her solution worked. Sister Dolores never had to deliver such harsh punishment—to anyone—ever again. And she never raised her voice.

Personally, Sister Dolores opened my mind. She suggested *David Copperfield* for my next book report—beginning a two-year quest to read all of Dickens' novels. At her suggestion I began a collection of short stories (I recently found the Spiral notebook I'd used to record them—lots of memories) that started me on my lifetime love of writing. She complimented the flower I painted when I thought I had no art talent. She made me feel special.

And interestingly, every other student who went to St. Raphael's that I've met in the years since feels the same way I do.

Sister Dolores began as my teacher. Turned into my mentor . . . Became my friend . . .

After Steve and I stopped in Missoula to visit her when we were engaged, she confided, "You did good, Darlene. He's a man, not a boy."

Over the years, either alone or with Steve, often including our daughters, I made sure to stop and spend an hour or two with her when we were close to where she was living/going to school/teaching—in Missoula, Great Falls, Spokane.

When Michele was first born, Sister Dorothy (after Vatican II, she'd reverted to her birth name), was spending the summer at Gonzaga graduate school while living at the nun's convent by Sacred Heart Hospital.

One summer evening, I drove to the convent to visit Sister. Baby Michele slept in her basket that sat on the back seat of our station wagon. After I parked and exited the car, ready to get Michele out, I watched in horror as our brand new Chevy rolled down the slight incline in the parking lot and headed toward the main artery in South Spokane. With my baby in it!

Thank goodness someone had parked in the car's path. While my car bashed in the side of the other vehicle, my daughter was safe!

In spite of it all, Sister and I had a nice visit. I have no idea what we talked about. I learned that night to always double check that my car was fully in *Park*. And I thanked God that, even being low on money, we'd gotten insurance.

As time went by, I enjoyed many *over-nights* at the nun's convent house. In Spokane for a meeting, back and forth on trips to Kalispell to visit my friend Phyllis, visits to grandsons studying at Gonzaga—no matter what

Chapter 22

the occasion, we always had a great visit. Our conversations were eclectic—from old times and friends to politics to flowers (Sister had a beautiful rose garden, and we used to enjoy visits together to the gardens at Manito Park).

Once, when we were living on Chambers Creek, Sister attended a meeting at McChord Air Force Base. We were thrilled to have her live in our blue and white upstairs guestroom that week. In the evening we enjoyed dinners in our dining room and dessert on our patio. And then I introduced my dear friend to one of the joys of my life—the solitude of just being in the presence of God by the rushing waters of Chambers Creek.

Unforgettable.

When my first book, *Under the Gallus Frame*, was published, Sister rejoiced with me. "I always knew you had talent," she said. "Great story!"

Her comment made me smile when I got a negative review by one of the men in Steve's Rotary group. "It's full of foul language—fallen women," he complained.

When I told Sister about it later, she said, "Your story's about miners in Butte, Montana for heaven's sake! You couldn't ignore the Red Light district. And I'm sure they didn't call someone a gol-darn whippersnapper when they got mad. You did *real* and did it well."

Steve and I were guests at Sister Dorothy's Fiftieth Jubilee celebration. Hundreds of people attended the Mass and reception. Talking to the attendees, each told us a story of their special relationship with Sister.

We were invited to the family dinner that evening. Since her immediate family was very small—one brother—her parents having passed long before—she included Steve and me. What an honor!

Her brother, a Montana priest, knew lots of Steve's old Butte classmates so it made for interesting conversations.

I especially enjoyed the pictures displayed of Sister in the two years she'd worked as a Boeing welder during WWII—when she lived what we all call *a life*. But she chose a different path—she entered the convent.

After teaching for decades, Sister spent many years working for the Spokane Diocese. Finally, she served as an assistant at two local churches. She retired to be a full-time caregiver—for five years—of her lifetime friend Sister Michele.

Sister Dorothy is now close to ninety-two. Legally blind and the veteran of seventeen serious surgeries, she's had to move to Emile Court—an assisted living facility the nuns own.

But she's feisty as ever. Recently, Steve and I tried to plan a good time for us to visit her in Spokane. We had a difficult time picking a day—Sister was busy for two weeks.

At this stage of my life, I've known Sister Dorothy longer than almost anyone else alive. She knows me well. Her friendship is a continual gift. I feel truly blessed.

Chapter 23

Wenatchee

We moved to Wenatchee in April. Our Fiftieth Wedding Anniversary was on August 18, 2006. The girls wanted to have a big party for us in Tacoma. We told them not to waste their money. "We'll celebrate alone."

They were insistent.

Steve wore a white tux rented from Mills Brothers in downtown Wenatchee.

I wore a white and gold silk dress.

When we were *rich and didn't know it*, Steve had a habit of buying me beautiful clothes at Andrew's, an expensive ladies store in Lakewood. He found he could go in the shop, say, "I want to buy Darlene a present" (birthday, Christmas, etc.), and they'd produce the perfect outfit.

When Steve's parents' Fiftieth Wedding Anniversary arrived, he out-did himself.

After my in-law's celebration, I folded up the dream dress Steve had bought me and put it in my cedar chest.

When I brought it out 17 years later and said, "How do you like this?" Steve beamed.

We were married—the second time—on the afternoon of August 18, 2006 by Father Lee Hightower—in the grotto at St. John Bosco's Meditation Park.

We'd belonged to the parish for almost thirty years. I'd prayed at Meditation Park both before and after Steve's 2002 cancer surgery. Steve had gone to high school with Fr. Hightower at Butte Boy's Central.

It felt like old-home-week. Friends and relatives came from all over.

. . . Dodo and Ray, niece Wendi, her husband Doug and baby Michael from Minnesota, Marty and Colleen Hackett (he was Steve's best man at our wedding—she had gone to college at Holy Names with me) arrived from Eugene, Oregon. Maureen O'Conner—our Butte friend who I'd worked with in both Tacoma and Louisville—flew up from Denver.

. . . Greg Andrews (son of my dear, dead friend Janet), his wife, and two daughters from Gig Harbor. Thelma and Daryl Plager (our Cascade Way friends now living in Redmond) and their daughter MaryBeth (Stephanie's childhood friend) and her husband and son.

. . . Sandy and Carl Luttinen—original Oakbrook friends—members of our Couple's Bridge Group—long time Lake Chelan Shores buddies who now lived on Bainbridge Island.

. . . Bob (my forever friend from Glasgow—now living in Covington) and his wife Pat. Their daughter Bobbie (who lived with us while she went to Bellarmine her senior year) and her husband Cubbie. And untold dozens from the local area.

We all met after the wedding ceremony at Oakbrook Country Club. I remember the thrill of dancing with the love of my life—dear Steve—as we had done so many occasions in the past.

It was a glorious day!

Steve and Darlene on their Fiftieth Anniversary

Chapter 23

That year—2006—the market began to weaken.

We watched in horror as our financial world crashed in 2007.

The last of our retirement savings evaporated. The value of our newly purchased house plummeted.

We looked for jobs. Steve got a position as a substitute-teacher at the Eastmont School District. But he wouldn't get his first check until November 1. I was unable to find employment.

We tried to sell our house—at a price much lower than we'd anticipated. No luck. The first of the year—our drop-dead date—loomed.

Finally, one night we were sitting on our front porch having a glass of wine before dinner when a car cruised by our place. Slowly.

Minutes later, we got a call from a real estate agent. "I've got some people who are interested in your house. Can we come over? Right now?"

They came. Walked through. Gave us a cash offer. Too low.

Steve negotiated. He won some issues—but not all. We lost our substantial down payment. Would have to start from scratch. *For the third time—I was counting.*

Steve got his first check from the school district November 1. On January 4, another tough move. Another cold. Tears of frustration. And loss.

We rented a lovely cottage. Moved in on January 4, 2008. It had covered porches in both front and back—a large room over the garage that I used for a combination office and sewing room—2400 hundred square feet. It wasn't *ours*, but I loved it. Loved the beautiful fireplace in the great room—the vaulted ceiling—the big master with two sets of double doors—the separate dining room.

We settled in.

On my birthday in May, I went to Mass at Holy Apostles. Afterwards Fr. Argemiro invited me to share coffee with him in the rectory kitchen. He asked me to fill the open position of church secretary.

I pondered. Prayed—a lot. Asked Steve's guidance.

Finally, I took the job—it began June 1.

The pay wasn't much—as I told a nosy parishioner who asked my salary—"It just about covers my cost of gas to drive back and forth."

I haven't mentioned this before, but, after 2000 when we moved back to Tacoma, I became an avid fan of the Gonzaga basketball team. I mentioned that fact to Phil one evening when he came from Spokane to take us out to dinner. (Phil was the Gonzaga alumni representative for Washington State.)

One afternoon shortly after our meeting, I returned from work to find the message machine blinking. It was Phil.

"I've got two tickets for the Gonzaga game at the Kennel tomorrow night," he said. "You want 'em?"

Basketball fan that I was, I started packing in my mind as I asked for details.

The next afternoon, Steve and I parked on Astor Street, a block from St. Aloysius Church. We wandered the college campus, hand in hand, as we'd done many Saturdays when we were courting—over fifty years before.

Inside McCarthy Center, we were alone in a crowd of over six thousand. Close enough to the court that we could hear the squeal of Nikes as the players dribbled up and down the hardwood. So near we could see the beads of sweat on their brows. But in the solitude of two.

After the game, the years disappeared as we walked back through the campus—beneath the stars. We stopped and kissed by the Ad Building, as we had done hundreds of times before. But now, we didn't have to end the evening with just a goodnight kiss.

We hurried to our hotel room and ordered a pizza. Then we got comfy, climbed in the king-size bed, and enjoyed wine, pasta, and each other. In that order.

It was magic.

⁓

I learned to love my job at Holy Apostles. I helped people—scheduled weddings, quinceaneras, and funerals. I managed the St. Vincent de Paul program to help the needy—we gave food vouchers, paid utility payments, and rent. And I listened.

I made friends with a large portion of our parishioners.

Steve and I made a good life for ourselves in Wenatchee. Then one Thursday in late May—when we'd scheduled a long weekend in Tacoma with our family—we got a registered letter from our landlord. He'd put our cottage for sale—given us a deadline to move—by July 1.

We had to hustle. There wasn't much available to rent—at least not a house where we could fit our furniture.

Chapter 23

Finally we settled for a place just a few blocks away.

It was as big as our Creek House—3,600 square feet on two levels, had a commanding view of Wenatchee, the river, East Wenatchee, and the eastern hills.

Bad thing—it was $400 more a month rent. And we had a breeder of hawks and peregrine falcons living with his birds next door. Lots of squawking and a bad smell when we had a southerly wind.

We entertained a lot—inside. We could take advantage of the spectacular view via the large windows.

Friends for dinner . . . The National Grand Director of my women's group and her traveling companion—two delightful women—for their annual visit to our YLI group . . . Our kids for a long Thanksgiving holiday . . . My church women's group for a potluck in early December . . . A big brunch before Christmas . . . We had fun.

After returning from Christmas in Tacoma with our family, we had a *Just us* New Year's Eve.

On January 5, 2011 our home was invaded.

While Steve and I were at work, the female part of our landlord duo came into our locked residence. Without notifying us. She had the gall to leave us a note.

"Couldn't find my mail. You must have it—it didn't come to our new place. By the way your place is lovely."

We were appalled!

Does she think that by telling us she likes how we've decorated, she can make herself at home in our absence?

We felt violated. After all, we'd paid for the privilege of living there.

Our income tax records sat on the top of the desk, out for anyone to see. She'd probably read every little detail.

After praying about what to do, we started looking for another house—maybe for $400 less monthly rent.

We found several. The ones we liked sifted through our fingers like sand. The last place—a two-bedroom loft apartment—we thought we had. The owner said, "It's yours. Unless some friends of ours happen to sell their house by the end of April." It sold the next day.

We pulled out all the stops—started a St. Jude novena.

Brown's Point

A few days later, a vendor came by the church office. We got to talking. He told me he and his wife just sold their house in Seattle and were moving into an apartment in a senior citizen complex in the Brown's Point section of Tacoma.

Hmm, I thought. That's halfway between Stephanie and Michele. I accessed the floor plan on the internet. Steve and I drove over that Saturday morning. Got a showing at 11 a.m.

It was small, but nice. The manager said they'd put in new carpet and vinyl, and paint all the walls. The complex was pleasant. Rhodys and azaleas bloomed everywhere. (I'd missed my Creek Place garden.) The manager would hold it for $450. We told her we'd think about it.

When we got back to Wenatchee, there was an unexpected check for $457 in the mail. "How much more push do you need, Darlene?" Steve asked. I sent Norpoint Village a check.

Michele and Stephanie each made a trip over and got what they wanted/could use. We had fun going through memories as they made their choices. We had an estate sale. Gave the rest away to the YMCA secondhand store and the church.

I must admit, I wept more than once as I gave up my treasures. The credenza we'd bought in 1967 with Steve's first bonus check from Allstate . . . Steve's roll top desk . . . The brass bed from our guest room . . . 86 classic books from our leather-bound collection . . .

And Christmas—it nearly devastated me when we had to part with two of my favorites—my trapunto and our Christmas castle (third edition)—there just wasn't room in our new apartment in northeast Tacoma.

The list went on. And so did we.

Our two bedroom apartment was small (especially after just moving from a 3600 square-foot house). But lovely.

We met Sib and Dave—they lived right across the street—two of the nicest neighbors we'd ever had. Sib invited me to join her for lunch at the Federal Way Women's Club. I became a member. Enjoyed their book club immensely.

We were there when our Michele got seriously ill.

When Stephanie and her son Jake went through the trauma of a contentious divorce, we helped as best we could. When Stephanie took on the jungle of her big yard—after five-plus years of neglect by her ex—we put

Chapter 23

on our work clothes and dug in. When Jake joined the Army, we saw him take his oath.

But back to the beginning of our Brown's Point experience . . .

When we were still in Wenatchee and in the throes of deciding whether or not to move to western Washington, my friend from work, Silverio, was going through a similar situation.

Originally from Colombia, Silverio had immigrated several years before to find a better life for his family. By the time I met him, he was a citizen, had obtained citizenship for his two children, and was in the process of getting a permanent visa for his wife.

In the almost four years I knew him, he spent thousands of his hard-earned dollars to *jump through the hoops* to facilitate his wife's move to Washington State. That spring, he'd lost his latest fight. Once again he'd been told *No* by immigration. Missing his family, he made plans to move back to Colombia.

While in the U.S., Silverio had gotten a car—a car that he needed to sell before he left.

Steve and I talked. We had two vehicles, a twelve-year-old pickup for my husband—a seven-year-old SUV for me—both happily free and clear (just the way I liked it).

"I'll sell my pickup," Steve said. "That way we can buy Silverio's car and give him a good sendoff. I'll drive Silverio's Civic to work. It'll be my work car—don't need anything fancy for that."

After the moving van left Wenatchee with our boxes and furniture, we filled both of our cars with the little stuff.

The Civic purred all the way to Brown's Point. On the way over Snoqualmie Pass my CRV developed what sounded like a bad cold.

In October, Steve began substitute teaching in the Auburn School District—about a half hour drive away. One afternoon I got a call from Steve after school. "The car won't start. Please come get me."

An hour and a half later, we got home. "Think I just flooded it," Steve said. "It'll be fine tomorrow."

The next morning when I dropped Steve at the school in Auburn, the Civic started right off. "Must have been a fluke," he said.

As I drove the CRV back home, my car's cold began to sound like bronchitis.

We repeated that scenario (Steve's car dying—me rescuing him) twice more—like we were practicing for a high school play and not quite getting it right.

But money was tight. We crossed our fingers and waited.

Then one November afternoon the Civic died in the QFC parking lot. Steve lifted the hood. Tinkered a bit. Finally got the car working.

"Darlene," he said, "we have to bite the bullet and get that damned car to the shop tomorrow."

I cowered in the passenger seat, trying to figure out how to pay for the unknowable.

Not a block away from the grocery store—as we approached the very busiest intersection in Federal Way—at 5 p.m.—the engine stopped.

Horns blared. Cars began stacking up behind us. A car full of teenagers passed us illegally on the right side making rude gestures and shouting obscenities.

I dove into the jockey box—got the phone number for our insurance "help" line—dialed. No answer.

Ordinarily I cry when I'm completely frustrated. Knowing Steve didn't appreciate such behavior, I bit my lip, stared down at my cellphone, and dialed again.

Suddenly I heard a tap. Taken aback, I looked up and saw five teenagers who looked like they were members of the local chapter of Hell's Angels right outside Steve's window.

Laboriously, Steve rolled down the side window (nothing was automatic on *that* car).

"Got a problem, Mister?" the leader asked. The nail-head skull emblems on the two front pockets of his jacket flashed a not-so-subtle warning.

Steve looked all around—saw no one else—no motorcycle gang ready to make their bones on him. He told them the basics of our distress.

The boys sprang into motion immediately. Two directed traffic around us—the other three pushed our car into the Three Bears gas station.

Before we could say a heartfelt *thank you*, our benefactors disappeared. Another guy got our car running.

"That was eerie," Steve said as we drove home. "Those kids came from out of nowhere." He paused. "You know I'm not really into the supernatural, but if I were, I'd say they were angels."

I nodded. "*Someone* was taking care of us, Steve. And I gotta tell you, I feel very blessed."

Chapter 23

The next day—Friday—Steve got the Civic running—went to school—with the intention of driving to the Honda dealer after classes ended. That afternoon I got a distress call from Steve. Drove to Auburn and picked him up. We left our sick car in the school lot.

On Saturday a tow truck pulled the Civic to the Honda shop. We sat there—worrying. Like we were in the hospital awaiting news about one of our kids who'd been in an accident.

When the mechanic came out he rattled off a bunch of things that were Greek to both of us. Finally he said, "It'll cost you as much to fix your Civic as it would to buy a new used car. For $973.87 we can get it running. However, the same thing will probably happen again tomorrow. We suggest you junk it."

I gasped. "You're telling me we should throw our three-month-old car away?"

The mechanic nodded.

Steve looked stern.

Although there were no crashing cymbals or drumrolls, we felt the change of atmosphere before we saw the new addition to the equation—the new-car salesman Charles.

"How 'bout I show you what we have in the showroom?" he said. "Just to give you some options."

In a daze, we followed.

"Like your CRV?" he asked. "How 'bout moving up to an Odyssey?"

I guess I didn't hide my gasp very well as I perused the cost sheet on the back window of the sleek, shiny black model Charles pointed out. He quickly moved us to a CRV. An Accord... A Civic...

Charles watched me like a hawk riding the thermals looking for prey.

"If price is your hot button, how 'bout a brand new black *Fit*? I've got one with your name on it out in the lot."

Before I could protest, I found myself in the back seat of said *Fit*, having a silent fit while Charles explained the Honda Fit's features to my upset husband.

"How 'bout if the two of you take a personal test ride—have a bite of lunch. When you get back, we can work out some numbers."

About that time I'd have done anything to leave Charles and his "How 'bout's".

Steve drove down Old Pacific Highway. We ate. Discussed our situation.

"I had no idea a new Honda would cost more than our Emerald Drive house," I whined.

"Get real," Steve said. "That was over forty years ago."

I finally confessed my worst fear. "I'm pretty sure the CRV is dying too. Sometimes it sounds like it's on its last breath. We can't afford one new car to say nothing of two." (Our budget didn't allow for *anything* extra.)

"Engine sounds good to me," Steve said.

"You need hearing aids," I reminded him. "Someone could drag me out of our bed while you were asleep beside me, and you wouldn't hear them."

After an afternoon of negotiating, we ended up trading in our CRV (Charles giving us a *generous* $1000 for the dead Civic? Yeah right!)—and getting a big monthly car payment for a brand new vehicle neither of us wanted.

The Fit never fit.

Then . . . Steve got sick. His first doctor said, "Probably nothing." He got worse.

The second M.D. gave him a prescription that didn't help—then suggested Steve see a urologist.

Steve made an appointment. Before the date came, Steve got a letter in the mail saying the urologist—Number Three—had quit his practice.

Giving the second doctor another chance, Steve got the name of new urologist—thirty minutes away from home—in Lakewood.

Steve saw this doctor—had tests taken.

We went to Lakewood for a consultation with Number Four. "It's prostate cancer," the doctor said noncommittally. "I need to do more tests to see how bad it is."

Steve had the tests.

Days later—Number Four called. "The tests are *not* good! I'll explain your options when you come in."

The first appointment Steve could get was in two weeks. We waited for what seemed forever. The morning finally arrived, and Steve and I drove the half hour to Lakewood to see the doctor. Every minute was its own agony—for each of us.

Chapter 23

What would the doctor tell Steve? You've got a month to live? You need surgery tomorrow?

Neither of us was optimistic.

We were early for his 8:30 appointment. No one was at the desk. At 9:00 a woman appeared. Steve stepped right up and was told, "Oh, the doctor won't be in today. Besides you have no appointment." (Steve had left the written confirmation notice home so we couldn't prove it.)

In desperation I asked, "When will the doctor be back?"

The nurse said, "We have no idea," then turned away, dismissing us.

"Please . . . Connect us with another doctor," I pleaded. "We're worried. We need to know how serious this new cancer is. Timing could make the difference." I didn't say "this is a matter of life or death," but I sure was thinking it.

Without an ounce of empathy, the nurse said, "No one else can help you. You'll just have to wait until the doctor comes back. Go home. Call back in a week or so."

We drove home in silence—30 minutes of unceasing worry.

When we got home, we both said the same thing at the same time, "What about Dr. Monda?" (A Wenatchee urologist who'd treated Steve's kidney problem and eventually removed Steve's right kidney in 2009.)

Steve called Dr. Monda's office. His nurse remembered Steve immediately—got him an appointment that Friday.

"Finally a real live doctor who's willing to see me right away. What a difference!" Steve rejoiced.

I must admit I didn't say anything for a few minutes—I was in shock.

Finally I decided to share something with Steve that I'd dismissed earlier in the month.

"Well, I guess this is as good a time as any to tell you," I said.

"Tell me what?" Steve almost yelled. (It *had* been a trying morning.)

"About the e-mail I got a couple of days ago from Roger. Remember him?"

"The owner of The Lofts in Wenatchee? What did *he* want?"

I nodded. "He wondered if we were still interested in an apartment."

Long story short—we warily looked at the one bedroom apartment on Friday. (Before we'd thought Roger's two-bedroom unit was too small). We liked it—rented it. Saw Dr. Monda who found Steve's cancer could be treated with hormone therapy.

Once more, I began packing.

As I packed, I thought. (I'd always done some of my best thinking while doing my least favorite chore—ironing.) (I also hated packing.)

After all the people who'd looked at The Lofts, how had Roger chosen us to contact when he had a vacancy? I'd met with him twice—Steve once. Not exactly what you'd call a compelling reason to choose one tenant over probably 20 to 30 on his wait list.

Synchronicity?

A miracle?

Whatever, I felt blessed.

Chapter 24

We moved back to Wenatchee on April 4. Immediately, we felt at home in our new loft. The day we moved in, the owners invited us—and the residents in the other three apartments—to a *welcome* party at their place—they lived right across the hall from us.

I started my exercise regimen immediately.

Five days a week, I still walk three miles. On Wenatchee Avenue, I turn at the Owl Soda Fountain. Walk the pedestrian bridge that curves over the railroad tracks and a busy road. Turn left when I get to the Columbia River. Then I follow the water on a winding paved path the local Public Utility District built when they developed a *nothing* into a park.

I pray the entire time. Prayers for my family—formal prayers and personal—petitions and thanksgivings.

I see a robin... A bald eagle... A blue heron... A newly opened pink dogwood... A rose...

And I see God in his creations. Hear Him. Feel Him in my heart.

Along the way I often meet neighbors—Cindy and Charlotte and sometimes Carla—Ben and Clara, with their baby in the stroller. New friends—Bernie and his wife, Marian and Lillian. And there are the nameless regulars. The Water Man. The lady who walks with two miniature Schnauzers on leashes. The humpbacked woman who clips right along and always says, "Hi." The young mothers pushing babies in strollers.

On the avenue, life bustles.

I love the Owl—they make milkshakes served in foot-high metal containers, just like those Uncle Henry bought for me when I was a kid. I walk past Mills Brothers Men's Store—in business well over 100 years—where my husband got the white tux he wore at our Fiftieth Wedding Anniversary party. Sometimes I stop at Mela to chat with friends having coffee at the outside tables.

I love Wenatchee!

Steve and I put down our roots. Like our freshly planted geraniums and two tomato plants, we grew. And flowered.

It was the end of summer—August 28, 2013. Other people complained about the heat—90 degrees at 2 p.m. I loved it.

Steve was scheduled to begin subbing the day after Labor Day—good for two reasons. The first of November we'd get a check from the school district—which would be greatly appreciated. And—I'd have some *alone time* to continue writing my book-in-progress—*The Bakken, Boom and Bust*.

Steve sat on our couch enjoying the air conditioning in the living room. I was making a batch of oatmeal cookies. Looking up, I saw he'd gone out on the deck.

Funny, I thought as I drew the beaters one more time around the bowl.

While measuring a cup of chocolate chips to finish the batter, I felt his presence. Felt. Not heard. He motioned to his throat. Gasped, "Can't . . . Breathe . . ."

I tore down the hall to my neighbor Charlotte's apartment. She's a nurse.

Charlotte took charge. She checked his blood pressure—210 over 136. Called our doctor—told her the details. Said, "I'm taking him to Emergency immediately."

At the hospital I watched a half-dozen gowned people bustle around my husband. They put an apparatus over his nose (breathing treatment they explained), poked him in the arm, and hooked him up to a big bag hanging on what looked like a rolling clothes hanger. They pasted at least a dozen white disks all over his chest (an electrocardiogram/EKG).

I waited in a corner, thankful they'd let me stay in the same room as Steve while they worked on him.

About five hours later, Charlotte drove me back home. They'd kept Steve overnight for tests.

Our place seemed eerily empty. I tried to act normal. Took out the bowl I'd hurriedly stashed in the refrigerator. Spooned the dough on the already-greased, aluminum sheets. Baked the cookies. (I'd not suggest waiting five hours to bake oatmeal cookies—they tasted *strange*. Ate them anyway.)

The next afternoon—twenty-four hours after his attack—without finding out what caused his distress, I drove Steve home.

"These cookies taste funny," he said.

Chapter 24

I laughed. Agreed. Said, "I'm just glad you're here—able to chew."

※

Steve began subbing after Labor Day.

※

One of the things I loved about moving back to the Apple Capital of the World was being able to rejoin the Wenatchee Valley Writer's Group. I'd first been invited to join these serious authors in October 2003 when I was writing *Under the Gallus Frame* and living in Chelan. The camaraderie inspired me and fed my soul.

We met in the board room at Banner Bank twice a month. One breezy, sunny afternoon—the second Friday of November—I was halfway to the bank, moving at a fast pace, when I saw something out of corner of my eye in the window of the YWCA Thrift Store.

My gosh, I thought. *That looks just like my trapunto—the one I made in 1980.* I stopped. Looked closer. Opened the door and went inside. One look at the backside told me, *It is mine*!

Quickly I checked my watch. Almost late, I hurried up the street, hoping no one else would buy it until I could come back and rescue the treasure I'd given away two and a half years before.

It was an extra-long meeting.

By the time I got back, the store was closed. But the trapunto was still in the window.

Hurray!

Steve was as excited as I was. We'd both lamented having to give it away when we down-sized prior to moving back to Tacoma.

First thing the next morning, we went shopping. Paid $21 for the treasure we'd thought had been lost forever.

"Can you imagine?" I marveled. "No one else bought it."

"Worth every penny," Steve said, "There's that synchronicity of yours working overtime."

Everyone we tell this story to says, "Proves you were meant to move back!"

Now, every Christmas, my well-loved trapunto hangs over our mantle, a reminder that miracles do indeed happen. Especially at Christmas.

We had a lovely Thanksgiving dinner as guests of dear friends.

The next day we got a notice from our health insurance carrier. They'd refused to honor Steve's doctor and hospital bills—all charges since we moved back to Wenatchee the past April 4. The total was *huge*.

Monday was a disaster. In phone call after phone call Steve kept saying, "We *did* change the coverage—the end of March—before we even moved."

It took until 2 p.m. before a manager promised, "I'll check."

Just before 5 p.m., I found Steve on the deck, bent over from the waist—gasping for breath.

I ran down to Charlotte's. She was gone.

Oh my God, it's all up to me!

Somehow I got him to the elevator—into our car—headed up Yakima Street to Central Washington Hospital, about two miles away.

I knew that Yakima Street was relatively traffic free. But I had three main thoroughfares to cross before I had clear sailing.

Wenatchee Avenue was no problem.

The light was green at Mission. I raced through.

As I approached Chelan Street, I saw yellow in the distance. It turned bright red as I arrived. I must admit, I thought of running the light. But when I looked to my right and saw three lanes of car lights coming at me, I stopped.

"Are you with me?" I pleaded as I looked at Steve. I heard a wheeze. Got a weak nod.

I swear, I could have cooked a hard-boiled egg before that light turned green. From then on—driving untraveled streets—I broke the speed limit. Big time.

When I got to Emergency, I stopped right by the front door. Got Steve out the passenger side. Abandoned my car.

Seeing a vacant wheel chair, I sat him down—quickly and carefully. I drove that thing right to the admitting desk like I was competing in a new Olympic event.

"He can't breathe!" I yelled. "We don't have time for your insurance mumbo-jumbo."

A nurse appeared from nowhere. Zoomed him through the closed doors marked *No Admittance*.

Only then did I allow myself to pray.

Please God, let Steve's insurance card work! (I *had* kept my wits about me enough to drop Steve's billfold in my purse.)

Chapter 24

The woman at the admitting desk was very kind. She asked his name and date of birth. And—miracle of miracles—his insurance information (albeit not including the terrible amount allegedly due) popped up on her computer screen. "I have all I need," she said. She didn't even need his proof-of-insurance!

Thank you, Lord!

Having gotten that taken care of, I hurried outside, hoping my car hadn't been towed away. Luck was with me. I said another *Thank you, Lord*, re-parked, and went back in.

By the time I got back to the room where they were treating Steve, he was already hooked up for sound. And turning purple.

No one told me anything.

Hours later, the doctor-in-charge appeared, stood directly in front of me.

"Don't you *ever* drive your husband here again when he's in the midst of an attack like he just had!" the ER doctor yelled. "He was dying! That's what ambulances are for!"

I hung my head.

After what seemed like forever, the doctor—in a normal tone—added, "Your husband's stabilized. We're going to keep him for observation."

The next day, they released Steve again saying, "We can't determine what's causing your problem."

The insurance company (thanks to a lot of nudging by our new Wenatchee health insurance agent) finally got things straightened out. We owed more than I'd hoped—by a lot. But it was thousands lower than their original amount. I negotiated a time-pay plan—a little bit every month. Forever—or so it seemed when I got off the final phone call concerning the problem. But we could go forward.

On December 23, Steve and I took the bus to Tacoma. Stephanie picked us up at the terminal—we were going to stay with her for a few days.

We spent a joyous Christmas Eve with our whole family—Michele and her boys, Larry and Sean, and Michele's Bill—at Stephanie's. We Skyped Jake—in the Army at Fort Bragg in North Carolina. We all missed him terribly, but enjoyed the ability to *see* Jake and actually talk back and forth. (And to think that in 1995 I'd actually said, "The internet will never work!")

Stephanie had an old family friend to Christmas dinner. A few others arrived to say "Hi." Lots of *stuff* about long-time secrets that Stephanie had suffered alone surfaced.

Steve and I were so happy we could be there for Stephanie that evening when everyone finally left. We've never felt closer.

At home again in our loft apartment in downtown Wenatchee, Steve and I had our long-time traditional *Us Only* New Year's Eve—good music (Sinatra and *I'm in the Mood for Love* by Rod Stewart)—fine wine (champagne for me—red for Steve)—home-cooked dinner (entrée by Steve and dessert by me.)

All seemed calm. Steve had started subbing again. I was working on my novel.

It was January 14, 2014. I was explaining what the dentist had told me at my appointment earlier that day when Steve abruptly staggered to the deck.

"Air," he gasped.

This time I didn't waste any time. I called 911. Or tried. My fingers wouldn't work.

I ran next door—to neighbors Clara and Ben.

Clara got the ambulance.

Because we live in a super-secure third floor apartment, getting the ambulance was a challenge. One key to get in the building, another for the elevator. Ben took charge.

The EMTs let me ride with Steve in the ambulance.

Ben got our car to the hospital and parked it, while Clara drove theirs to bring them both back home. Their twelve-year-old babysat the two younger daughters.

This time Steve did not come back the next day. A half-dozen different doctors did God-only-knows-how-many tests.

I prayed. Worried. Prayed some more. Worried.

What's the matter? I agonized.

Finally, on January 22, one of the premier heart surgeons in the Northwest operated. Did a three-way bypass. We'd had no idea Steve had heart problems.

Chapter 24

I'd called the family when I got the diagnosis. Michele was in the middle of problems of her own. Stephanie immediately informed me, "I'm coming."

I told Steph, "I can do it myself."

She ignored me. Came. I really appreciated her just *being there*.

The operation took six hours. My rosary beads were almost smoking by the end.

Dear Charlotte, who worked in the operating room, came down to give us a head's up every hour or so.

Both Stephanie and I breathed a sigh of relief when Charlotte came the last time and said, "All went very well. He's in recovery."

Steve looked terrible when we first saw him back in his room. Like a ghost. He was wired for sound.

"My God!" Stephanie cried. "Will he make it?"

I assured her, "He'll be fine, Steph. I've seen your dad a dozen times when he's just gotten out of recovery. He's a fighter. And a good healer."

I started counting: "his first kidney surgery in 1958, a torn rotator cuff in 1997, four colon cancer surgeries in 1998, another in 2002.

"While we were living in Chelan—two skin cancer surgeries, two inner ear surgeries, and two kidney stone lithotripsies.

"When we got to Wenatchee, two more lithotripsies, an exploratory kidney surgery that led to having his right kidney removed, a hernia, and two cataract operations.

"In our two years back in Tacoma he had two more skin cancer surgeries and a major prostrate scare that ended up with our moving back to Wenatchee."

I stopped for breath.

"That's twenty-two if I'm not mistaken. Plus his tonsils, knee surgery, and appendectomy before we even met.

"Dad and I have kidded about the scars on his body," I continued. "His torso looks like a patchwork quilt sewn by a half-blind beginner."

Somehow, after my soliloquy, the mood lightened.

"I get the picture," Stephanie said. "Dad's going to be fine."

Lots of people came to see Steve at the hospital: Father Rolly and Deacon Pete (our Croatian buddy). Heart bypass survivors from our church—Bob and Donna—brought stories of healing. My friend Roxanna dropped by several times. Our Loft neighbors Jay (another cardiologist) and wife Karla stopped to say "Hi."

Michele called several times. Dodo sent a cheery bouquet and roses arrived from grandsons Larry, Sean, and their dad Larry.

I almost lived at the hospital.

Steve had a beautiful private room (all the rooms in this almost-new hospital were private) that had an actual single bed built into the window seat. You could sleep there easily—pillows and blankets were provided—heated if you liked. I napped on that bed a bunch, but went home every night to sleep.

I clocked how much time it took me to drive—normally—from our door to the hospital. Just seven minutes.

I wondered, *How long did it take me—that night?*

I heard an answer, *You really didn't drive, Darlene. You were carried.*

Two days after his surgery, Steve was walking up and down the hospital halls. He was released on January 26—five days after his three way bypass.

My husband is amazing!

Thank you, God!

Darlene and Steve after Steve's surgery

Chapter 24

A few days after Steve got home, he told me this story.

"One minute I was lying on the bed in emergency. The next I was being propelled down a brown tunnel. I had no idea where I was going, but I wasn't a bit scared. In fact, I've never felt so at peace. I didn't want it to end."

That weekend Deacon Tom (a cardiologist besides being a deacon) stopped by, and Steve told him about the brown tunnel.

"You were on your way to heaven, Steve," Tom said. "I've heard that story before. You were called back. You must have more to do here."

Steve was back subbing on February 18.

I can't swim. Yet I mentally treaded water that February.

I knew the bills for Steve's heart surgery would begin coming in. Soon! Remembering his colon cancer surgeries in 1998, I also knew that it would take months before the insurance would be settled. And, since we'd changed our health insurance on January 1, I had no idea how good our coverage was—what I would eventually face.

I worried.

Steve has called me a world-class worrier. (And that is *not* a compliment.) Years before, disgusted, he challenged me, "Go sit in a corner, Darlene, and don't come back until you worry up some money."

Needless to say, I didn't go sit in that corner because I knew what I'd come up with—nothing.

As March approached, I remembered another time in my life when I had a problem—1955.

That spring I'd really needed help. My high school boyfriend Mike had quit Gonzaga after only completing one semester (*after his folks borrowed the money for his second semester tuition from my parents*). He was back in Glasgow living (*sponging?*) on my folks (*bunking in a former motel unit they now used for storage*).

Mike had been gone from Spokane for six weeks. I was torn as to my feelings.

What should I do? I prayed as I sat in St. Al's the first Sunday of March.

And I got an immediate answer—*Go to the Novena of Grace.*

What in the world is *the Novena of Grace?* I asked.

I got my answer—from the pulpit. The Novena of Grace—dedicated to St. Francis Xavier—is a nine-day period of concentrated prayer to God for one's most important intentions. It was beginning at St. Al's that coming Friday.

So I trudged the four blocks from my dorm to St. Al's—twice a day for nine days—to plead to St. Francis Xavier—through the Novena of Grace. I agonized over exactly what my request should be. I finally decided on this:

Please, make the right thing happen to my relationship with Mike.

Soon after the novena ended, I went back to Glasgow for Easter vacation. Mike had changed—or I had. What had once been a romance—so sizzling we were planning to get married after we graduated from college—had become as cold—to me—as yesterday's mashed potatoes.

Soon after I got home, my mother took me aside. After all these days, the moment and the message are still burned into my heart. My mother and I were standing in our kitchen—between the sink and the refrigerator.

"Mike's got this big idea—he wants Daddy and me to co-sign with him on a bank loan." She explained the idea. I listened. Digested it. Thought—only a moment. Said, "No, don't do it."

And I went back to Spokane.

Days later I met Steve at that never-to-be-forgotten mixer.

The March after we were married Steve told me he'd gone to that very same Novena of Grace. He shared his request. "I prayed for a wife. And right afterwards, I met you."

After 60 years, it hit me—Steve and I got married—and are still together—because our prayers were answered during that long ago Novena of Grace.

I thought of the synchronicity that had appeared out of nowhere.

A miracle? Absolutely.

Chapter 25

THAT SUMMER WE TOOK a couple of short trips.

Kalispell . . .

We stayed with my Glasgow friend, Phyllis and her husband Bill. Enjoyed delicious meals, great conversation, and the beauty of being so close to the majestic Swan Range it felt as if we could touch the mountains themselves if we just leaned over the rail surrounding their deck a bit more.

Phyllis and I shared memories like sisters. Bill and Steve encouraged us.

This trip Phyllis surprised me with a gift from her dear mother (who had just passed away the previous fall)—three leather bound volumes of *Footprints of the Valley*—a history of the remarkable people who populated Valley Country where we grew up.

When I got home I read stories of hundreds of families—ones I knew—others I got acquainted with as I read. I finally got to show Steve a picture of Mrs. Friedlund, my piano teacher for ten years, a true lady I remember with much fondness.

Footprints of the Valley was a priceless gift!

One day while Steve and I were visiting with Phyllis and Bill, we drove over to the next town—Columbia Falls—where we visited with Steve's Uncle Curly (Rudy Matule) at the Montana Vet's Home.

Although Curly could hardly see and we had to yell to talk, we found him to be sharp as a tack. While it was interesting to hear him intelligently compare the various 2014 cars, I enjoyed his stories of being a Marine more. Steve and Curly had kept up a brisk four-year-old correspondence from 1942 through 1945. But after he came home, Curly pulled a heavy shade over those years.

Now he couldn't tell us enough. He'd been a sergeant in the Fourth Marine Division. Fought at Saipan, Tinian, and Iwo Jima. He told us of watching, a bayonet away, as a photographer took the iconic picture of the American flag being raised on Iwo Jima. Curly donated his Purple Heart to the Montana Veterans Home—it sits in a place of honor in the display case as you enter the building.

We left with great memories of a lovely day—and a well-loved copy of Curly's photo-history of the *Fourth* marines. We will treasure it always.

I believe Curly and Steve loved each other like father and son.

He died on March 6, 2015—one-hundred-thirty-three days short of his one-hundredth birthday.

Steve spent a day with college friend John while Phyllis and I *did* the resort town of Whitefish.

I can imagine the stories they told. (Steve was Vice President of the Gonzaga Student Body the year John was President—1956-1957.)

The newest story, however, was that of John's recent illness and *cure*.

For months, he'd been forced to use either a walker or a wheelchair. John and Margie had been back and forth to the Mayo Clinic in Rochester, Minnesota seeking help.

Then, when they were back at the clinic for his umpteenth checkup, the doctor asked John, "What's your goal? What do you want to get from this treatment?"

John thought for a moment and said, "What I'd really like is to dance with my wife."

This spiked the doctor's interest. He found that—when newly married—John and Margie had danced to the live music of Tommy Dorsey. The physician fiddled with his cell phone a minute and came up with Tommy Dorsey band music.

John told Steve how he got up, left his walker behind, grasped Margie's hand, and they danced.

That Sunday we met John and Margie at St. John Paul II Church in Bigfork. The priest was Father Donald Shea—he and Steve grew up neighbors in Butte's Dublin Gulch. Father Shea told us how the whole parish had prayed for John's healing—and now rejoiced together.

After Mass, John and Margie and Steve and I had brunch. After eating, Margie showed us a video on her cell phone of John walking with his walker before the incident—slowly, a jerky, uneven gait. Then of the two of them dancing—like they were kids again.

Chapter 25

"A miracle?" Perhaps . . . It sure looked like one to me. Whatever, John is still walking. By himself. And dancing with Margie.

Lakewood . . .

Our next trip began one morning in late June when we left our home in Wenatchee bound for Sea-Tac airport.

I was first in line when Jake deplaned. Steve stood in the distance—just far enough that the big *Welcome home Jake* sign he held stood out for all to see. It was the first time we'd seen our youngest grandson, now twenty, since the day he'd enlisted in the Army, on Steve's birthday, April 1, 2013.

Now, on furlough before deployment to Afghanistan, we cherished the time we had with Jake.

Stephanie gave a big party in her backyard.

I made an ice cream cake—Jake's favorite.

Our grown-up grandsons Larry (and his girlfriend Katey) and Sean (and his girlfriend Catherine) came from Seattle. Michele and Bill from Issaquah arrived.

And Stephanie's friends joined us—she has tons. Her new friend, Larry DeGagne, brought his mother and father—Louise and Patrick.

It was a good day.

We spent another good day with Jake exploring Lakewood. With Steve and me having lived in Lakewood for thirty-three years, and it being Jake's only home before he joined the Army, there were lots of memories.

We saw Jake's old haunts. Drove around the new Lakes High School—where both of our daughters and all three grandsons graduated. Drifted past our old homes (I'm an unapologetic lover of *all* my homes—each and every one).

Finally, Jake brought us to Chambers Bay (site of the 2015 U.S. Open golf tournament). We got out and walked a large part of the eighteen holes. Located on a large bay on Puget Sound, the view is spectacular. You can see forever. The Narrows Bridge looms to the north—Steilacoom to the south.

The finale was fireworks.

Actually, Stephanie planned an evening for the four of us at Cheney Stadium watching the Tacoma Rainiers. But, hard as I try, I can't remember either the team we played—or who won.

I *do* remember the color that blazed on the midnight blue sky—I can see it in my mind's eye nine months after—the most beautiful fireworks show I've ever seen. Multiple rockets burst simultaneously for at least a half hour. A particularly bright display would end. I'd think, *That's it*. But no, it would be followed by another. And another. And another.

Jake attended dressed in his uniform—it was *Honor Our Troops Day*. Everywhere we went, people stopped to greet him, wish him well, and tell Jake how proud they were of his service.

How appropriate! Our Jake was on his way to serve with the U.S. Army in Afghanistan upon his return to Fort Bragg.

Chapter 26

ARMED WITH GOOD VIBES, I finally dared make a trip I'd been avoiding for eighteen years.

I left my daughter Stephanie's house—walking. Turned left on Phillips Road . . . Walked . . . Prayed . . . Remembered . . .

At Turquoise Street I stopped.

Should I really do it?

I'd left our creek house on April 25, 1996—mentally kicking and screaming. Twenty years of my life, I'd lived in my dream home—loved every minute of it. But fate had ordained we move halfway across the country—to Louisville, Kentucky. It promised a new chance.

I'd found fate sometimes lies.

That July morning, I followed my heart.

I felt dwarfed as I made my way down the narrow road. Douglas fir trees towered on either side. Just past the mail boxes, I turned right when a sign on a fir tree declared: *Creek Valley Lane.*

The memories flooded in so fast I thought I might drown.

I remembered the January day when it snowed so heavily that driving down the steep, curved drive to our home would be inviting disaster. Carrying two grocery sacks full of food (one containing a bottle of wine that chilled as I walked), I'd avoided the areas where I'd seen ice that morning. Yet, at times, it felt like I wore ice skates instead of leather-soled shoes. When I'd finally maneuvered down the slippery, windy road, I found there was no electricity—in our all-electric house.

When Steve had arrived, he made a fire in the fireplace, enclosed our family room with heavy blankets in both doorways, and made a snug haven for us. We sipped our wine while sitting on the hearth, cuddled close to stay warm. Loved each other.

Another day, Steve walked to the mail box, retrieved our morning paper, and came back with a bundle of wiggly, ivory fur. We gave the beautiful Lhasa Apso he'd found abandoned at the end of the road a special name—Snicklefritz. Our vet friend warned us she was already old—probably ten years. She quickly became a part of the family. We cherished her for five love-filled years.

Snick should have taught me a lesson—enjoy while you can. Alas, I'm a slow learner.

When a bird's song interrupted my reverie, I lifted my eyes skyward. Saw a lone robin. The sight reminded me of the newspaper ad that had lured us to Oakbrook originally—a robin red breast sitting on an oak branch. The caption below heralded the message: *Your noisiest neighbor.*

I welcomed the noise.

Next, the memory surfaced of watching robin babies peck their way out of four robin-blue eggs in a nest mama had made in a tree right out of our second-floor bedroom window.

I smiled.

Walking slowly, I immersed myself in the moment.

One part of me wanted to catch a ride on a ray of sunlight and magically return to the past.

Another looked for closure.

As I made the final turn, I hurried toward the gentle roar of rushing water. Stood on the narrow bridge over Chambers Creek, looking to my right. There it was—the beautiful two-story home Steve and I had created together. Almost like making a baby, our dream home evolved from our imagination to fruition in less than nine months. In the morning light, it looked like a cover on *Sunset* magazine.

I remembered the many photos our across-the-creek neighbor Norm had taken from his viewpoint—shared with us. One winter scene was so spectacular it prompted us to use it as our Christmas card that year.

I had to reach into my pocket for a tissue.

Blood, sweat and tears? Yes, we'd given all three for the privilege of nesting in our valley home for twenty years.

To save money in making our audacious dream a reality, Steve and I made a deal with the builder. We'd do all the painting, wallpapering and cleanup for a discount on the final cost. Little did we know what *all cleanup* included.

Chapter 26

The property was heavily wooded. We'd wanted to retain as many trees as we could. But just to clear the footprint of the house, they removed a good dozen giants. Steve remembers watching the bulldozer *attack* a tree, keep at it until it fell on the ground—the huge stump exposed—and then push the whole thing, trunk, branches, stump and all—onto our extra lot. By the time the bulldozer finished, we had a pile of debris as high as our two story house that filled the area for sixty feet between the road and the creek.

We thought the builder would take care of cleaning up the mess.

"No way," Leo said, "That's part of cleanup."

Inquiries to landscapers about the cost of removing the rubble would have given a less dedicated couple a double heart attack.

After research, we found that the most economical way to deal with our problem was to burn the whole shebang—one stump at a time.

"So," Steve tells the (absolutely true) story, "I lit one match on Memorial Day and started a (controlled) fire that never went out until Labor Day."

We started small, hacking our way into the extra property five feet from our new house. Some of the over-a-dozen stumps, many of them hidden between felled brush and hundreds of branches from downed Douglas fir and cedar trees, were taller than my husband and easily five to six feet in width.

Word-of-mouth advertising of *free firewood* brought several men with chainsaws down our hill to cut up the downed trees for their woodpiles. A win-win situation for both them and us.

Steve used his brawn to move the big stuff. I picked up what I could. My work often found me on the ground where I became well acquainted with a local monster—the black slug—a five-inch slimy creature that I hated with a vengeance. I freely confess to stabbing every single one I found with a twig and roasting it on the hottest spot in the fire.

We slaved like pioneers that entire summer. I even gave up my every-Saturday appointment with my hairdresser (for me a BIG thing).

Steve was forty-two that summer—I'd just turned forty. Forever after when we approached a job that proved to be tougher than we'd anticipated, we'd both laugh and say, "Well, you can tell we aren't forty anymore!"

The next summer had been the fun part—buying and planting dozens of rhododendrons and azaleas and hydrangeas. The result—a showplace garden. I remember one rhody we got on sale at Ernst Nursery for ninety-nine cents. Only twelve inches high when we planted it, I christened my find *Ninety-Nine*. (In twenty years, it grew so high that my tall husband had to climb a ladder to debud it in the spring.)

We'd turned our acre-and-a-third into a park. Our adopted mother and dear friend Lynn called it our *es-tate*.

Now, as I approached our once-in-a-lifetime-wonderland, I winced. The entrance that had once looked like a mini-Butchart Gardens was now a disaster. Dozens of rhodys had been pulled out—replaced by nothing but weeds.

I trespassed. Walked off the road a few feet so I could get a better view. Happily the lilac bush Michele had bought me one Mother's Day still stood where I'd planted it—uncared for—but there.

In my mind's eye, I saw a bouquet of the purple flowers I loved in the middle of the kitchen table. But I knew I hadn't taken time that last April to gather a fragrant bunch of lilacs. I'd been too busy. Cleaning. Trying to make my soon-to-be abandoned home look like it had been inhabited by fairies who never set their feet down—not Mrs. Clean and her husband.

All of a sudden I realized, *I never said goodbye. Maybe that's what had been haunting me for so long.*

I started giving up ownership that minute. Instead of inhabiting my dream house, I'd make a documentary of my past. One I could keep with me always.

Giving thanks for my combination of almost flawless memory and a good imagination, I began assembling a video in my mind of what had been my heaven-on-earth for twenty years.

I stood at the edge of the sunken area Steve had created with huge rocks and brawn and turned into a croquet course. Happy memories of games with daughters and grandsons.

Mesmerized, I watched a kingfisher sitting motionless in a tree. It seemed like hours before the right moment arrived. I saw him swoop down, dip his beak under the water, and fly off with his lunch.

I put that recent tidbit in my movie. Added long-ago sightings of blue herons and blue jays, of ducks—mallard and merganser. Of wildlife—brown bunnies and raccoons. Highlighted the morning I saw mama and papa raccoon and their three babies walking on their hind legs right up to our front door—like they were coming to visit.

Glancing to an upstairs bedroom window reminded me of another special moment—the morning I'd spotted a three-and-half-foot river otter

Chapter 26

playing in the creek. His lustrous brown pelt glistened as he dove into the water and emerged a few yards away. I clicked. Captured that memory.

It had been years, but I couldn't forget the fall return of salmon up Chambers Creek to their spawning ground. Sometimes we'd be privileged to watch one actually burrow into the gravel of the creek bed right in front of our eyes.

When I came to the house itself, I was surprised that I had no urge to go up to the front door, knock and say, "Hi, I'm Darlene. I used to live here, and I'd really like to take a walk through." (I'd actually done that once in Spokane at our third home.)

Why? I asked myself. I'd agonized for years about what the new owners had done to the place I'd loved so much and had to leave.

Now—suddenly—my memories sufficed.

What a relief! Could it be I was cured?

I turned toward my entry point. Began walking. Stopped here and there. Let the ambience of each individual place seep into my being. Like osmosis.

Gingerly, I walked over the bridge for the second time that day. Got as close as I could to the edge. Made sure I had the very best view of the creek side of our old place. Clicked the camera in my mind.

I flew up the windy road. As free as a butterfly.

In total, by the time I got back to Stephanie's, I'd walked two miles. I checked my watch—I'd been gone for two hours.

A feeling of peace enveloped me like a big hug. I knew that I'd never again feel the agony of loss that I'd experienced for so long.

I was healed.

Chapter 27

It's April 2015.

Nine months have passed since we said goodbye to Stephanie and Jake that July morning. Nine months—the gestation of a human.

Steve and I—long past the age of procreation—have lived the last nine months—simply.

He's learned how to play the melodica, substitute-taught dozens of classes, and thus did his bit to educate the local twelve to eighteen-year-olds in the Three R's—and the plain old life skills of honesty, diligence, and the joy of achievement.

I've finished my novel *The Bakken* and begun the sequel *The Octopus*. I'm looking for a publisher and working with my ministries.

Steve's had a super report from his urologist—his PSA (a prostate cancer indication) has plummeted down from twenty-three to under one.

Both of us have suffered from ordinary life ills. Steve had the flu I call *The Crud*. I fell and sprained my right wrist and thumb—negating my ability to make homemade cinnamon rolls for Christmas—the first time I missed since I began in 1959.

We've enjoyed our friends and neighbors. Watched our beloved Zags make it to The Elite Eight. Worshipped at our church—Holy Apostles.

We haven't won the lottery or the Nobel Peace Prize.

But we're living. Loving each other.

With a big day almost here—the Sixtieth Anniversary of Our First Date—I began to think. How? Why us?

And I thought back to one of my favorite quotations by the renowned mountain climber, W. H. Murray.

> *Until one is committed there is hesitancy, the chance to draw back, always ineffectiveness. Concerning all acts of initiative (and*

Chapter 27

creation), there is one elementary truth, the ignorance of which kills countless ideas and splendid plans: that the moment one definitely commits oneself, then Providence moves too.

All sorts of things occur to help one that would never otherwise have occurred. A whole stream of events issues from the decision, raising in one's favor all manner of unforeseen incidents and meetings and material assistance, which no man could have dreamt would have come his way.

(from *The Evidence of Things Not Seen*—Baton Wicks Publishers)

And—suddenly—I saw the truth.

When Steve and I met sixty years ago—and were joined in a sacramental marriage sixteen months later—we *committed* ourselves to each other.

Then *Providence* moved.

And all sorts of things occurred to help us make a life that we could never have dreamt would have come our way.

So I began to write our story.

www.ingramcontent.com/pod-product-compliance
Lightning Source LLC
Chambersburg PA
CBHW051925160426
43198CB00012B/2038